In Darkness Light

The Millennium before the Reformation:

How God preserved His people during the Dark Ages.

*In His death and resurrection,
Jesus drank in darkness and spit out
light.*

*The people who walk in darkness
Will see a great light;
Those who live in a dark land,
The light will shine on them.*
Isaiah 9:2

In Darkness – Light!

The Millennium before the Reformation: How God preserved His people during the Dark Ages.

by Stuart L. Brogden

Printed in the United States of America

ISBN 978-0-9986559-6-3

PUBLISHED BY:

Brogden's Books
https://baptistlibrary.6te.net/Books.html
brogdensbooks@gmail.com
La Vernia, TX 78121

All -Scripture references are from the Holman Christian Standard Bible (HCSB) unless otherwise noted.

Table of Contents

Endorsements

In our day it truly is not a necessity that the faithful Christian be gifted with acumen akin to the men of Issachar to adequately assess the egregious demise of sound doctrine within the evangelical church at large. Whether by ill-guided disregard or by the designed assumption that doctrinal emphasis serves to produce a soporific irrelevancy with the pews, evangelicalism is plagued with biblical ignorance.

Directly connected to this biblical, doctrinal ignorance, acting as a compelling catalyst for it and producing a reinforcing effect for continued neglect, is an overt obliviousness of biblical and church history. Scripture is, for those to whom it is more than a mere pietistic, verse-plucking devotional tool, an abundant proof of God's sovereign control of history. That history includes past history, as revealed within its pages, current history, and future history. God controls, produces, and providentially organizes it all. The cliche is simply not simplistic ... history is "His Story."

The book you now hold, *In Darkness - Light!*, provides the church with a sorely needed glimpse into an era of sovereignly orchestrated history which many only know as the Dark Ages. What author Stuart Brogden wonderfully shows, however, is that for the redeemed of God, the darkness of the times did not represent, to them, a disregard by their faithful God. Brogden delves into the tumultuous challenges, doctrinal attacks, and often outright hostility which the faithful faced during this time. He shows the sustaining grace of the Lord and

His providential guidance in the midst of an ecclesiastically turbulent time.

Brogden's work is amply documented, allowing for further study, appropriately polemically incisive, and provides the reader with two appendices of dire importance. In the first, a presentation of the church's historic, orthodox creeds is supplied, and, in the second, a helpful assessment of the nature of the church is given. *In Darkness - Light!* deserves to be devoured by the faithful for encouragement in our own times, and as a rich record of the truth that history is the Lord's. This book boldly affirms that He is utterly faithful to His own, even in times when it superficially seems to be otherwise. Brogden has here given the church a much-needed resource. May the faithful glean wisdom from it, and may their faith be bolstered by it!

Bud Ahlheim
https://podcasts.strivingforeternity.org/show/the-bud-zone/

"Standing upon the Word of God and refusing to accept a higher authority as demanded by the Roman priesthood, Hus was despised by that entire power structure. The most dangerous activity in a totalitarian society is thinking. The religion of the world requires submission; the gift of God is liberty that no man can take away." (page 133) All through church history, from the end of the book of Acts until the present day, God has had a remnant of people who through His divine Providence have been exposed to the truth of His word and had it applied to their hearts by the Holy Spirit.

The average modern Christian has very little knowledge or understanding of the struggle that has taken place over the last two thousand years as the light of truth of God's word has continued to radiate salvation by grace alone through faith alone in Christ alone in and through the suffocating darkness of dead works religion. In this book brother Stuart Brogden has peeled back the veil of history to give us a glimpse of the work of the Spirit of Christ in His people keeping the torch lit and bringing the truth along with unprecedented liberty of conscience to God's people in this present day. May we be stirred up, emboldened, and led to worship by this encouraging testimony of light!

M. Paul Priest
Pastor/Elder Heritage Baptist Church
Lake Charles, LA

I have always been interested in Church History. Throughout all the centuries of this world, God has had a remnant who are His people. No matter what persecution and heresy the people of God have endured, our great sovereign God has directed it all, to the smallest detail of His design, for His glory! Truthfully, in all Darkness, the Light of the Lord is seen. This book is a wonderful addition to my library, and I recommend it to laymen and scholars alike.

Tom Lassiter
Elder, Crestview Baptist Church
Big Spring, TX

I highly recommend *In Darkness-Light!* by Stuart L. Brogden. This insightful and thought-provoking book sheds light on a period of Christian history that is often overlooked or misunderstood - a time when the true gospel message was threatened by Catholic dogma.

Through meticulous research and engaging prose, brother Brogden reveals how God was faithful to preserve the gospel light, through his remnant, in the darkest of days.

The author's extensive knowledge of theology and history vividly illustrates the triumph of the kingdom of light over the forces of darkness. If you're seeking a book to enhance your comprehension of the Christian faith and the gospel, this is an exceptional option that is strongly recommended. It is a necessary read for those who wish to delve into the abundant past of Christianity and acquire a new outlook on the history of the Church.

Robbie Jeffries
Pastor, Rye Patch Baptist Church
Ludowici, GA

Too often, the focus of volumes written on the era called The Dark Ages is isolated to the spiritual bleakness. By contrast, Stuart Brogden's *In Darkness – Light!* displays to the reader the faithfulness of our God, who promised to preserve His church in all eras, and did exactly that. Introducing us to key characters and movements that stood upon and battled for the truth, the author shows that our Lord at no time ever failed to keep that promise, maintaining a people for Himself in the world. *In Darkness – Light!* also provides an accessible read to all, as it is briefer than many more exhaustive treatments of that vast span of 1,000 years - but while not exhausting the reader with the gloom of how dark those times were, but rejoices in the grace and light that was still present despite the strenuous efforts of the enemies of the gospel to quench it!

Dennis Gundersen
Board member of Tlapaneco Indian Ministries, Guerrero, Mexico; author of *A Praying Church* and *Your Child's Profession of Faith*

How God Preserved His People During the Dark Ages is more than merely a sub-title, it is the essence of our preserving God who calls us out of darkness, enlightens us in the midst of darkness and provides the light for others in darkness. Stuart Brogden's use and explanation of the early Creeds is not intended to supplant Scripture, but to aid in enlightening the minds of Christian truths for those who, at the time, did not have access to printed bibles as we have today. Thus, the entrance into the Dark Ages.

There are those who, as Stuart states, "bridged the Dark Ages to the Reformation". Jon Hus, for example. Stuart presents a riveting portrayal of this great man of God, enduring the darkness of evil and illumined by Holiness. He survived the popery, relentless persecutions which extended to all who dared to give Hus aid. An interesting irony is pointed out in this chapter wherein while Hus was imprisoned by the Pope, another (ex-

Pope) termed the (anti-pope) was captured and thrown into the same prison. We read much about Christian persecution but few of us actually experience it to the point of imprisonment and/or death. Hus lived the very words of our Lord to live in the light of God letting our light shine in the darkness around us.

Spiritually speaking, the world of fallen humans is a dark place indeed. While we walk in the light as the redeemed elect of God, we must pity and pray for the reformation from our dark ages as God calls us to live in the light. *In Darkness – Light!* is far more than a pithy term. It is a call for Spiritual renewal and commitment to serving God. Stuart Brogden has made plain the reason why, we were once in darkness but, *In Darkness – Light!*

Sam Hughey
https://www.reformedreader.org/index.html

II Corinthians 4:4 says, *"To who the god of this world hath blinded the minds of them which believe not, lest the light of the glorious gospel of Christ__who is the image of God, should shine unto them."* This tactic was fully displayed during the Dark Ages before the Reformation. However, true believers and those who fought the darkness with the gospel's light were also there. To document and illustrate the darkness and light during this troublesome time is a jewel.

Stuart Brogden has done the work on documenting these people and groups. He describes in vivid terms the heroes and villains during this crucial period. Brogden uses sources and scripture to indicate the struggle between the darkness and light of the time. It is an encouragement that the light will always win if we continue to shine it continually.

The material Brogden offers is very valuable in illustrating the hypocrisy of darkness and the courage of those who stood against its power, reinforced by the corrupt state religion. I highly recommend his book and believe it can be very helpful as a great source and road map for standing against the darkness of sin and ignorance with the light of the gospel and authority of God's Word. I hope the book inspires you to stand with God's truth as they did.

Dan Nelson
Baptist Historian, pastor, and author of 5 books, including *Baptist Biographies and Happenings in American History* and *Early Baptists: A Comparative Study of the Anabaptists and English Baptist Movements*.

In Darkness – Light!

Introduction

Thy Word is a lamp unto my feet and a light unto my path. (Psalm 119:105)

The Bible describes redemptive history in finite detail and in broad, sweeping terms; with light emerging from darkness as time rolls on. From the darkness of the void, God spoke light; yet He was, even before creation knew Him. From the darkness of a sin-cursed world, God spoke to Moses from a burning bush and gave him the light of truth. God's people rose and fell with each generation, showing how futile man's efforts are to make himself acceptable to the Creator. After a long silence from God, a spiritual darkness of 400 years, God sent the light of the world to bring life to the dead.

This pattern repeated in Scripture, with varying details, many times and it has been repeated with much diversity in the history of man since the canon was closed. With the advent of the printing press in Europe in 1452, the Bible was Gutenberg's first book; and the Word of God was unleashed on a people who had been living in a very dark age.

Post tenebras lux is a Latin phrase translated *Light After Darkness*. It appears as *Post tenebras spero lucem* ("*After darkness, I hope for light*") in the Vulgate version of Job 17:12. Reformers are fond of the phrase, *Post tenebras lux,* to refer to the light of the gospel that spread across Europe in the 16th and 17th centuries. Too little attention is paid to the providential care YHWH consistently had for His people during the Dark Ages.

1

My goal for this book is to help the saints see God at work in the dark times, using the Dark Ages as the stage. We are called to walk by faith, not by sight (2 Corinthians 5:7); we need to train ourselves to trust God when everything around us looks dark.

With many professing Christians embracing sin, calling homosex and abortion gifts from God, it may appear we are in a very dark time. God is still God; Christ Jesus is still the only refuge from sin and evil and God's wrath. When Christ was crucified and buried in the tomb, the disciples thought all was lost; they were in their darkest hour. Yet on the third day, He burst forth in glorious light and He lives forever more! As the women at the tomb were told, when they looked therein and did not see Jesus: *remember His words* (Luke 24:1-8). This is still the right counsel for God's people: we cannot see Jesus, but He is ever with us. Remember His words, abide in His truth, trust in His Spirit, and shine like lights in a dark night with the God's truth.
Selah.

The Dark Ages was a millennium, running from approximately 500 (Rome fell in 476) to 1500 AD (Martin Luther's 95 Theses were written in 1517); being a three-fold darkness: spiritual, physical, and educational. "One must be accustomed to the light, at least in some measure, to be able to judge of the darkness. A blind man can have no idea of the extent of the darkness around him. It is the same as to moral and spiritual darkness. A person must have some acquaintance with the light of scripture in order to discern the darkness around him. Thus, alas, during the

2

ages under consideration, it was indeed dark, as it had been when our Lord was on earth: *The light shineth in darkness; and the darkness comprehended it not.* (John 1:5.)"[1]

The growing influence of the state-church kept the Scriptures locked up in Latin. The invasion of Europe by Muslims made living quite chaotic for many, lowering standards of living across the continent. Famine, plagues, and the general lack of medical understanding meant many died in their prime, further impoverishing families. These things combined to make learning all the more difficult and, over time, completely out of reach for most people. The Roman Catholic religion emerged in the first few centuries of this era, taking advantage of every crisis and causing several of their own (such as the Crusades) to enhance their power. Andrew Miller, in his book *Short Papers on Church History*, repeatedly pointed out that the papist religion was fit only for an ignorant and superstitious people. As the Dark Ages dawned, far too many people were lost in a spiritual darkness that was far more dangerous.

In 2012 and 2013, I spent time in Oradia, Romania and Florence, Italy. Both of these cities have several ancient cathedrals built by the papist and Eastern Orthodox religions. In each city, at buildings of each of these cults, I saw countless people walking as if zombies, lighting candles and bowing robotically before a statue or framed picture of one of the "saints" they recognized. I was struck at how much these people reminded me of those souls who play in the casinos all night long -

---

[1] George Morrish, *Darkness of the Dark Ages*, Introduction

which one cannot avoid if in Las Vegas, as the hotels are designed so one has to walk through the casino to get from the guest room to the convention hall or meeting rooms. Spiritually dead people going through their traditional routines.

This review of church history is selective. It must be, by the very nature and historical setting of the subject. It is also somewhat subjective, as no writer is able to be neutral. My intention is to provide a concise, competent overview of this period of time, with an eye on seeing the hand of God on His people. This book is full of quotes from authors (one of whom, Karl Adam, is an apologist for the cult of Rome) who painted a better word picture than I am able to do. I've worked to weave a narrative together around these quotes, providing a consistent, progressive picture of the history in question. The work we should admire is that of God, not that of any author trying to shine His light on history.

I am not interested in trying to prove a fleshly connection back to any biblical mortal person, as the body of Christ is a spiritual organism and does not rely on fleshly procreation but on supernatural regeneration.

There has been no documented evidence of clear succession of physical churches from apostolic times to present day; making such attempts rather pitiful - as if the Lord had not clearly revealed that fleshly connection with those in our past does not constitute the kingdom of God. There is adequate historical evidence to show God's people were active in every generation we have knowledge of; built up by knowledge passed down and wisdom given by God. There is no benefit for the saints of the living God to claim John as our father by fleshly connections any more than there was for the ancient Jews to claim Abraham as theirs. Cunningham observed, "His church, though not always appearing in a visible organized form, has never been destroyed from the earth. He has always had a seed to serve Him, - placed, it may be, in great variety of outward circumstances, living some of them within the pale of very corrupt churches, but still holding His truth, and walking in His ways."[2]

My prayer is that this book would reveal the one true God as the One Who does all things well and has promised that not one of His sheep will be lost. Even in the darkest times, YHWH sees all, directs all – for the good of those who love Him and are called according to His promise.

I am your unworthy servant,

Stuart L. Brogden

Author of *Captive to the Word of God, The Gospel In Isaiah,* and *The Gospel In Romans.*

May you be strengthened with all power, according to His glorious might, for all endurance and patience, with joy giving thanks to the Father, who has enabled you to share in the saints' inheritance in the light. He has rescued us from the domain of darkness and transferred us into the kingdom of the Son He loves. (Colossians 1:11-13)

---

[2] William Cunningham, *Historical Theology*, ch 16

In Darkness – Light!

1. The Early Creeds.

So we have the prophetic word strongly confirmed. You will do well to pay attention to it, as to a lamp shining in a dismal place, until the day dawns and the morning star rises in your hearts. (2 Peter 1:19)

The full text of each of the creeds discussed below is found in Appendix 1.

The people of God have never been without controversy over what Truth is. Much of the Bible is full of teaching God's Truth and exposing error, as Paul's two letters to the saints in Corinth show us. After the close of the canon of Scripture, those called out of darkness into the glorious light of Christ (Colossians 1:13) continued to fall into error and false converts continued to draw saints aside from the narrow way.

1 Corinthians 15:3-8 stands as creed of the faith; a written declaration of what God's people are to believe.

> *For I passed on to you as most important what I also received:*
> > *that Christ died for our sins according to the Scriptures,*
> > *that He was buried,*
> > *that He was raised on the third day according to the Scriptures,*
> > *and that He appeared to Cephas, then to the Twelve.*

7

> *Then He appeared to over 500*
> *brothers at one time;*
> *most of them are still alive, but*
> *some have fallen asleep.*
> *Then He appeared to James, then*
> *to all the apostles.*
> *Last of all, as to one abnormally*
> *born, He also appeared to me.*

The Christian faith is based on historic facts revealed in Scripture, made real to us by the Holy Spirit. We must be diligent to fight the battle in our own souls to hang onto the gospel and not drift away into error. Our flesh, the world, and the Devil are actively seeking to make shipwrecks of our faith. We must always be on guard.

Since man tends to always want something new to see or hear (Ecclesiastes 1:8), he clamors for a new revelation to satisfy this fleshly desire. Faithful servants of God, guarding the sheep against wolves, rose up and published specific responses to the error that had been brought into the fellowship, leading saints astray. We know many of these creeds, but perhaps have not considered why each one was written. We will take a quick trip down this stream of history to get a sense for the error being addressed and reaction to it.

The Apostles' Creed is the earliest known post-biblical creed; first circulated orally as the "Old Roman Creed" in the second century, emerging in written form in 351 AD. This creed was not written by nor, as far as history knows, spoken by the apostles. It does align with what was written for us by the authors of Holy Writ, although the phrase "He descended into hell" needs clarification. Contrary to the doctrine of some Word-of-Faith heretics[1], Jesus did NOT descend in hell after His death on the cross; He went that day to be with His Father in Heaven (Luke 23:43). Since the creed is not Scripture, we don't have to reconcile Scripture to it. The only reasonable way to take this statement is to see as referring to Jesus' being placed into the earth during His burial, knowing that "hell" often refers to the grave or the garbage pit near Jerusalem.

The statement in this creed mentioning "the holy catholic church" does not refer to the popish religion (which was not known to the world until much later) but to the universal body of believers. The word "catholic" means universal; when papists use this word with a capital "C" they claim their religion is the universal religion of mankind. The creed is right in its use this word, the papists are not.

This creed emerged, in part, to refute Marcionism, a gnostic-like view which held to several heretical teachings. Marcion taught that the Old Testament Scriptures were not authoritative for a Christian, denied that the God of the Old Testament was the same God presented in the New Testament, and that Jesus was the Son of the God of the New Testament but not the Son of the deity described in the Hebrew Scriptures.

We see why the Apostles' Creed emerged: the teachings of Marcion are heresy indeed and must be refuted by the saints of God. There is one God, the Holy Trinity, pre-existent and unchanging in His character and being; revealed in the old and new testaments.

---

[1] Joyce Meyer, *The Most Important Decision You Will Ever Make*, page 36

Yet this creed, like all the writings produced by mere men, must be tested in light of Scripture (1 Thessalonians 5:21). Children of God are to be disciples of Christ and not of men (1 Corinthians 1:12), no matter what our favorite author writes.

The Creed of Nicaea (A.D. 325), was written mainly to refute Arianism; the teaching that Jesus was not eternal, but created. The doctrine of the Holy Trinity was at the heart of the Creed of Nicaea. This creed was the product of what was called the First Ecumenical council of Nicaea, convened by Emperor Constantine. The council met to deal with the schism created by Arianism, an over-reaction to the heresy of Sabellius, who believed in a divine nomad which presented itself as Father, Son and Holy Spirit. Arians saw the Son distinct from God entirely, claiming he was a creature having a beginning: "There was when he was not." The Son was God's first creation Sabellius taught, yet out of nothing and hence has preeminence over the rest of creation. Arianism was an early form of the heresy of Modalism, still favored and taught by One-ness Pentecostals.

The First Council of Constantinople, (A.D. 381), modified the Creed of Nicaea by adding a phrase in support of the eternality and deity of Christ; refuting Apollinarism, which taught that Jesus had but one nature. Apollinaire taught that Jesus did not have a human spirit. His views were based on the platonic tripartite view of human nature. The council condemned this view in order to show that Christ, as truly human as well as truly God, could redeem the whole person.

The *filioque* clause (clarifying that the Holy Spirit proceeded from both the Father and the Son) is one of the major disagreements between the Eastern Orthodox religion and others which profess Christ. This is the creed recited in churches, and is still needed.

The Council of Chalcedon (A.D. 451) met to resolve the Monophysite controversy, which Eutyches stirred up by denying the existence of two natures in Christ. The two natures of Jesus, fully man and fully God, is a mystery not fully revealed to nor comprehended by man. That we cannot fully understand something given to us in Scripture is no excuse to deny it. The Definition document issued by the council summarizes the Church's teaching on the natures of Christ, and rightly specified the scope of Mary being the "God-bearer" - only as regards Jesus' humanness. Even so, the dispute about the two natures of Jesus continued until The Second Council of Constantinople in 533.

Council of Orange (A.D. 529). The Council of Orange was a further response to the 4th century controversy between Augustine and Pelagius, which had to do with the degree to which a human being is responsible for his or her own salvation and the role of the grace of God in bringing about salvation. Pelagius taught that human beings are born in a state of innocence, denying any sinful nature or original sin. This led many of his followers to believe man could attain a state of sinless perfection in this life. The Council of Orange dealt with the Semi-Pelagian doctrine that the human race, though fallen and ruined by a sinful nature, is still "good" enough to be able to lay hold of the grace of God through an act of unredeemed human will.

The Canons of the Council of Orange is a much longer document than the earlier creeds, covering much more

11

ground than the Pelagian heresy. With many words comes opportunity for error, men being yet sinful. The Canons are biblical and solid, yet we find in its Conclusion that grace is received in water baptism and that "all baptized persons have the ability and responsibility, if they desire to labor faithfully, to perform with the aid and cooperation of Christ what is of essential importance in regard to the salvation of their soul." No religious rite can impart divine goodness or righteousness to a human. This is a heresy (embraced by the papist cult) in an otherwise good and solid creed. We are still to "*test all things, hold to that which is good.*" (1 Thess. 5:21)

Athanasian Creed (ca. A.D. 500). This creed is seen as perhaps the best defense of the doctrine of the Trinity in abstract metaphysical terms, building on Augustine's definition of the Trinity. Each person of the Trinity is fully divine, unique to himself. Each is within the other, in perpetual intercommunication and motion, coequal and coeternal. The creed pronounces damnation for those who do not accept this teaching. The Athanasian Creed claims that it, in total, must be accepted if one is to be saved (becoming a member in the catholic/universal fellowship of saints). While nothing in this creed is contrary to the Scriptures, the Word of God does not teach that each and every doctrine presented in this creed is essential to salvation. The same caution about the word "catholic" applies as with the Apostles' Creed.

Anathemas of the Second Council of Constantinople (A.D. 533) The Second Council of Constantinople was called to resolve questions raised by the Definition of

Chalcedon, the most important of which had to do with the unity of the two natures of Jesus Christ. The Second Council confirmed the Definition of Chalcedon, while emphasizing that Jesus Christ does not just *embody* God the Son, He *is* God the Son.

The anathemas include a statement that Jesus was "twice begotten, the first before all time from the Father, non-temporal and bodiless, the other in the last days when he came down from the heavens and was incarnate by the holy, glorious, God-bearer, ever-virgin Mary, and born of her" (paragraph II). The Scripture tells us, *In the beginning was the Word, and the Word was with God, and the Word was God. He was with God in the beginning.* (John 1:1-2) In paragraph VI, the anathemas declare that Mary was the God-bearer in the fullest meaning of that term, claiming this was what Chalcedon meant; pronouncing anathemas on any who do not agree. "God-bearer" literally means "the one who gives birth to God," which is why the papists use the term "mother of God" in their scheme to elevate her. As John 1 reveals, Jesus is God and cannot stop being God, nor was there a time when He was not God. When Jesus was incarnated as a man, He was God. In a very strict sense, Mary bore God in her womb and can be rightly called Theotókos, the God-bearer. But, since He is God, He did not come into being at a point in time and His deity was not incarnated in Mary; she is not the mother of God.

Two more examples of why we need to carefully consider things written by man - even those written long ago and esteemed by many.

Third Council of Constantinople (A.D. 681). Spurred by the rise of the Monophysites, who taught that Jesus

13

had but one nature, this council further clarified the Definition of Chalcedon to deal with the question of whether Jesus had two separate wills, one for each of His two natures. Some people taught that, even though Jesus had two natures, He had only one will. The Third Council of Constantinople rejected this view as being too close to the teaching of the Monophysites, the council's report is an effort to thread the line between the Monophysite and Nestorian heresies.

I think it's clear from the account of Jesus in the Garden of Gethsemane that He had a human will, as He prayed, *My Father! If it is possible, let this cup pass from Me.* Yet He consistently did the Father's will, as His next breath reveals, *Yet not as I will, but as You will.* (Matthew 26:39) He came to do the will of the Father; we find this described in John's gospel: "*For I have come down from heaven, not to do My will, but the will of Him who sent Me. This is the will of Him who sent Me: that I should lose none of those He has given Me but should raise them up on the last day. For this is the will of My Father: that everyone who sees the Son and believes in Him may have eternal life, and I will raise him up on the last day.*" (John 6:38-40) This salvation required Jesus to drink the cup of wrath due each and every person that will be raised up on the last day. *My Father! If it is possible, let this cup pass from Me. Yet not as I will, but as You will.* Two natures, two wills, one person – the eternal Son of God.

There are other creeds, but these are the earliest and they show us a common basis for their existence: to make clear certain doctrines of core Christian belief and expose particular heresies with very specific language that would not allow vague statements or those contrary to accepted and proven Christian theology to stand. The later confessions (which tend to be much longer than the early creeds, espousing a far broader range of topics) appear to have much in common with the historic creeds of the faith. They were concerned with core doctrines and identifying those who embraced them as orthodox Christians, rather than politically active radicals seeking to overthrow the state.

As the Dark Ages spread across Europe, these early creeds and council declarations would provide guidance to some of God's people. Yet they also would be used to provide false support to state-church organizations that would emerge as the apparent face of Christianity.

If only I could be as in months gone by, in the days when God watched over me, when His lamp shone above my head, and I walked through darkness by His light! (Job 29:2-3)

In Darkness – Light!

2. Entrance into the Dark Ages.

"This, then, is the judgment: The light has come into the world, and people loved darkness rather than the light because their deeds were evil. For everyone who practices wicked things hates the light and avoids it, so that his deeds may not be exposed. But anyone who lives by the truth comes to the light, so that his works may be shown to be accomplished by God." (John 3:19-21)

Several names loom large in history, providing some insight to what was happening as the God of providence moved Europe towards the Dark Ages.

Constantine the Great was born around A.D. 280 into a wealthy family and became the sole Emperor of Rome in 324, having waged war against the western and eastern emperors. During a campaign to Italy against Maxentius, Constantine took time to ponder how he might gain victory.

> Constantine, though a wise and virtuous heathen, was a heathen still. He knew what he had to give battle to; and while considering to what god he should betake himself for protection and success, he thought on the ways of his father the Emperor of the West. He remembered that he prayed to the God of the Christians and had always been prosperous, while the emperors who persecuted the Christians had been visited with divine justice. He resolved

therefore to forsake the service of idols,
and to ask the aid of the one true God in
heaven. He prayed that God would make
Himself known to him, and that He
would make him victorious over
Maxentius, notwithstanding all his
magical arts and superstitious rites.[1]

Constantine had a dream in which he claimed Christ
Jesus appeared to him and gave him a visible sign to
guarantee victory. He professed to be a Christian,
though he held tightly to many of his pagan religious
practices and delayed water baptism until his death bed,
having the common but superstitious belief that water
baptism provided forgiveness of all sins committed up
to the point of baptism.

Constantine believed in the state as the bearer of
religion because it directly reflected and
expressed the divine will for the world in human
society. … In the Church of the Twelve Apostles,
which he had built, Constantine prepared in the
midst of the twelve symbolic tombs of the
apostles a thirteenth, for himself. Did not the
conversion of the empire fulfill the prophecy of
the apostles? This thirteenth tomb gave rise to the
emperor's title as "equal to the apostles."[2]

When Constantine issued the Edict of Milan in A.D.
313, Christianity was legally tolerated, no more a target
of civic persecution. In commenting on this Act of

[1] Andrew Miller, *Miller's Church History*, page 172
[2] Bruce L. Shelley, *Church History in Plain Language*, page 154

Toleration implemented by Constantine, Phillip Schaff remarked:

> But the spirit of the Roman empire was too absolutistic to abandon the prerogative of a supervision of public worship. The Constantinian toleration was a temporary measure of state policy, which, as indeed the edict expressly states the motive, promised the greatest security to the public peace and the protection of all divine and heavenly powers, for emperor and empire. It was, as the result teaches, but the necessary transition step to a new order of things. It opened the door to the elevation of Christianity, and specifically of Catholic hierarchical Christianity, with its exclusiveness towards heretical and schismatic sects, to be the religion of the state. For, once put on equal footing with heathenism, it must soon, in spite of numerical minority, bear away the victory from a religion which had already inwardly outlived itself.

> He exempted the Christian clergy from military and municipal duty (March, 313); abolished various customs and ordinances offensive to the Christians (315); facilitated the emancipation of Christian slaves (before 316); legalized bequests to catholic churches (321); enjoined the civil observance of Sunday, though not as dies Domini, but as dies Solis, in conformity to his worship of Apollo, and in company with an ordinance for the regular

consulting of the haruspex[3] (321); contributed liberally to the building of churches and the support of the clergy; erased the heathen symbols of Jupiter and Apollo, Mars and Hercules from the imperial coins (323); and gave his sons a Christian education.[4]

From all that history records Constantine did, I find nothing compelling me to believe his was a true conversion. History being somewhat – very! – fuzzy, we must be careful in being dogmatic about some things.

Bruce Shelley, a firm believer in Constantine's conversion, tells us, "He allowed Christian ministers to enjoy the same exemptions from taxes as the pagan priests; he abolished executions by crucifixion; he called a halt to the battles of gladiators as a punishment for crimes; and in 321 he made Sunday a public holiday. Thanks to his generosity, magnificent church buildings arose as evidence of his support of Christianity."[5] Constantine certainly supported the state religion that Shelley calls Christianity. We see how Constantine valued the Christian faith, as Shelley tells us, "After Nicaea, however, first Constantine and then his successors stepped in again and again to banish this church man or exile that one. Church teaching too often depended on control of the emperor's favor. The court was overrun by spokesmen for some Christian party."[6]

---

[3] A diviner in ancient Rome basing his predictions on inspection of the entrails of sacrificial animals. https://www.merriam-webster.com/dictionary/haruspex
[4] Phillip Schaff, *History of the Christian Church*, Volume III, Page 29
[5] Shelley, 100
[6] Ibid.

Slowly, ambitious men in the professing church gained favor with the professing Christians in state government; Constantine's sons did not embrace their father's professed religion nor his toleration of it. Yet Christianity became socially acceptable and many professing Christians became disciples of "the church" rather than of God.

> Whatever Constantine's motives for adopting the Christian faith, the result was the decline in Christian commitment. The stalwart believers whom Diocletian killed were replaced by a mixed multitude of half-converted pagans. Once Christians had laid down their lives for the truth; now they slaughtered each other to secure the prizes of the church. Gregory of Nazianzus complained, "The chief seat is gained by evil doing, not by virtue; and the sees belong, not to the more worthy, but to the more powerful."[7]

When the Reformation emerged, the magisterial reformers kept the state-church and people largely became disciples of those men. Christians who dared follow the Bible, as regards baptism, local autonomy, and ecclesiology, were hunted down and killed by these, much as they had been by the cult of Rome during its inquisition. The last murder of Baptists for lack of conformance to the state church in England took place in 1612, as Bartholomew Legate and Edward Wightman were burned at the stake for "heresy." Persecutions by the state and her churches continued for decades.

---

[7] Shelley, 127

John of Antioch was given the name Chrysostom after his death, in recognition of his "golden mouth" given to him by God for the proclamation of the Gospel. He was born about A.D. 354 into a wealthy family and studied public speaking as a young man. But he soon found worldly subjects did not satisfy his inner man, as if YHWH was giving him a hunger for the Word. He retreated into a life of austerity until the Bishop of Antioch promoted him to be a presbyter. In 398 John was appointed as Bishop of Constantinople, where he went to work to reform religious life to the Word of God, with preaching, prayer, and much exhortation. As with Paul the apostle, he went from synagogue to synagogue with the Gospel of grace with mixed results. John was hated by some (the rich and comfortable) and loved by others (the poor and common).

John spent the last several years being dogged by powerful religious men who hated that he was so popular among the common folk. This is a common thread, as it was in the day of Christ: people love power and when anyone or anything threatens their position or possession of power, they respond with venom. Men of God do not seek the applause of men, though they may get some honest encouragement from the saints. Men of the world covet the applause of men, even if it is coerced. John of Antioch died in his fifty-third year of age, in A.D. 407, weary of the conflict which flesh cannot win.

Augustine of Hippo was born in A.D. 354 to a Christian mother and a pagan father. His parents were not wealthy but did manage to send this son off to get a solid education, which culminated at Carthage, where he taught rhetoric and was highly regarded. In 383 he left Africa for Rome, which quickly led him to a teaching role in Milan; considered the de-facto capital of the Western Roman Empire. Things did not go well for Augustine and, after two short years in Milan he returned to his home where he was pressed into service in the church at Hippo in 391.

Many know that Augustine spent his early years as a dedicated hedonist; this public display of his depravity was a prime reason he was sent to Carthage for schooling. He got involved with Manichaeism in his teen years but apparently was converted during his time in Rome. This might explain why his teaching was less palatable in Milan than in Carthage and for his being drafted to serve the church.

Augustine was made bishop of Hippo in 395, spending the last years of his life in that position. He spent much energy exposing false religion, including Manichaeism, Pelagianism, and Donatism. This latter became a high-profile public controversy which was finally put down as heresy by a council in Carthage in the year 411. In opposing the Donatists, Augustine was initially opposed to coercion, but "he came to accept the use of force in a religious issue. What looks like harsh action, he said, may bring the offender to recognize its justice. Had not the Lord himself in the parable said, "*Compel them to come in*" (Luke 14:23)?

Thus, Augustine's prestige was made for those in later ages who justified the ruthless acts of the Inquisition against Christian dissenters. ... Augustine rejected the Donatist's view of a pure church. Until the day of judgment, he said, the church must be a mixed multitude. ... To support this idea, he appealed to Jesus' parable of the wheat and tares (Matt 13:24-30), overlooking the fact that Jesus was not speaking of the church but of the whole world."[8] His dispute with Pelagius continued until 418, when Pelagius and his disciple Celetius were excommunicated and condemned by a council of bishops. "Up to the time of Constantine, history offers no conclusive evidence that the bishop of Rome exercised jurisdiction outside of Rome. Honor, yes; jurisdiction, no."[9] Augustine died in 430.

Many books over many topics were written by Augustine, revealing the theological journey he was on. Papists embrace some of his writings, leaning on him for support of the doctrine of Mary's perpetual virginity, which leads to their idolatrous devotion to her. Christians embrace some of his writings, leaning on him for support of doctrines on man's depravity, predestination, and God's sovereignty. We should learn from this that no man is worthy of our undiscerning devotion.

Of *Augustine's City of God*, completed in A.D. 436, Schaff wrote: "In the present order of the world the two cities touch and influence each other at innumerable points; and as not all Jews were citizens of the heavenly Jerusalem, so there were on the other hand true children of God scattered among the heathen like Melchisedek and Job, who were united to the city of God not by a visible, but by an invisible celestial tie."[10] Here is the golden thread that binds all saints to the Lord Jesus; we

---

[8] Shelley, 137
[9] Ibid, 145
[10] Schaff, 76

have unity of soul with all the saints regardless of any fleshly connection or lack thereof.

John W. Kennedy, in his book *The Torch of the Testimony*, is among several authors describing the early dark ages as a time when the power and influence of the Romish Church was spreading and the people of God were growing - but not in the same way as the cult on 7 hills. I am reminded of a story from the saints in Communist China, known as the sermon of the broken glass.

Despite what one reads in the news, Christianity is basically illegal in Communist China. The government's Three-Self Movement, alone, has government sanction. Parents cannot teach their children the Bible until the children are 18 years old. Bibles must be those approved by the Three-Self Movement, which makes sure no King of kings is shown to be higher than the communist leader. And no more than 5 Christians can meet unless at an official Three-Self building. So, saints meet at times and in places where they can normally escape notice of the state. If they suspect a spy from the state is in their midst, the man who is to speak the Word will stand in front of the group, and say nothing. He will look intently at the saints and throw a glass to the floor, breaking it. He will then stomp on the broken glass, scattering fragments such that the glass can never be reassembled and then sit down without speaking a word. This sermon reflects what happened when Saul of Tarsus persecuted the saints and many of them fled to the far reaches of the known world, far beyond the reach of the Pharisees.

In Europe, people not satisfied with the Scriptures nor the approval of God found ways to twist Scripture in order to construct a new order to feed their egos, setting one group of people above others.

> The separation of a privileged class — a sacerdotal order — is unknown in the New Testament. The distinction between clergy and laity was suggested by Judaism, and human invention soon made it great; but it was episcopal ordination that established the distinction, and widened the separation. The bishop gradually assumed the title of Pontiff. The presbyters, and at length the deacons, became, as well as the bishops, a sacred order. The place of mediation and of greater nearness to God was assumed by the priestly caste, and also of authority over the laity. In place of God speaking direct to the heart and conscience by His own word, and the heart and conscience brought direct into the presence of God, it was priesthood coming in between them. Thus the word of God was lost sight of, and faith stood in the opinions of men. The blessed Lord Jesus, as the Great High Priest of His people, and as the one Mediator between God and men, was thus practically displaced and set aside.[11]

Pope Duncan argues that, contrary to the normal flow of history, the fall of Rome reveals a people of "the highest culture and the highest standard of living of any people the world had ever known" being over-run by "peoples

---

[11] Andrew Miller, *Miller's Church History*, page 146

who were not far removed from primitive man."[12] On the other hand, the Germanic tribes that conquered Rome had tribal social organization and no written language.

> In the year 435 Theodosius II commanded the temples to be destroyed or turned into churches. There still appear some heathens in civil office and at court so late as the beginning of the reign of Justinian I. (527–567). But this despotic emperor prohibited heathenism as a form of worship in the empire on pain of death, and in 529 abolished the last intellectual seminary of it, the philosophical school of Athens, which had stood nine hundred years. At that time just seven philosophers were teaching in that school. ... in general, it may be said that the Graeco-Roman heathenism, as a system of worship, was buried under the ruins of the western empire, which sunk under the storms of the great migration. But although ancient Greece and Rome have fallen forever, the spirit of Graeco-Roman paganism is not extinct. It still lives in the natural heart of man, which at this day as much as ever needs regeneration by the spirit of God. It lives also in many idolatrous and superstitious usages of the Greek and Roman churches, against which the pure spirit of Christianity has instinctively protested from the beginning.[13]

The struggle against state-churches began as soon as they began to emerge, as people of God will resist and

---

[12] Pope Duncan, *The Pilgrimage of Christianity*, page 39
[13] Schaff, 59

the state-church will always attempt to force non-conforming saints to submit; with the sword used in myriad ways to obtain physical conformance. The spirit of the child of God is not so easily constrained by exercise of force by fellow humans.

Before the dawn of our dark millennium, the Pelagian controversy raged. Early in the 5th century the doctrines of grace were examined, in an attempt to expose and correct the errors of Pelagius. The Council of Ephesus, A.D. 431, condemned Pelagianism without specifying the errors therein. Semi-Pelagianism begins to emerge, but did not gain formal acceptance - was even condemned by the Council of Orange in 529; yet it became the dominant view among professing Christians during our millennium - until the Reformation.

Although Augustine's defense of the doctrines of grace were not officially accepted by any early church council, his teachings had wide influence; helping God's people to resist the siren call of humanistic theology that would dominate Europe for a thousand years.

> Mr. Isaac Taylor, in the second volume of his *Ancient Christianity*, has proved that what he calls Demonolatry, or the religious worship and invocation of dead men, prevailed largely in the latter part of the fourth and in the fifth century, and was sanctioned by the most eminent men whom the church then contained, and even by Augustine himself. This had sprung up so readily, though by a gradual process, from the veneration paid to martyrs in the earlier period, and it is so natural to the mind of man, when true religion is in a

decaying state, that it came to prevail almost universally in the church, without giving rise to any controversial discussions which might mark the stages of its progress. There can be no doubt that, in the fifth and sixth centuries, there prevailed largely in the church a worship which might be fairly called polytheistic, and on which the monotheism of Mahomet was a decided improvement; though there is no sufficient evidence of the introduction of the formal invocation of saints into the public and prescribed services of the church till the seventh century.[14]

When the enemy attacks the saints, scattering them, they will take the gospel with them - taking the life-giving message of Christ to people they would not have otherwise met. And their enemies can never gather them up again to punish them. That is the sermon of the broken glass.

So it was when Saul scattered the saints, so it was when Rome did so. Yet, as Kennedy notes:

> The fire of the Spirit, however, was not quenched, nor can it ever be, and there remained those in the mountains of Caledonia and elsewhere, separate from what the world at large recognized as the Church, but maintaining their witness and refusing to accept the mediation of any human institution between themselves and God. These faithful people, and those who came after them, were

---

[14] Cunningham, chapter 12

29

to incorporate their faith in the spiritual movements of a later day. The torch of their testimony continued to burn, and was to be taken up in succeeding centuries to burn with a much brighter light.[15]

On this note, we enter the Dark Ages, with a look at what shaped the culture.

The term Christianity had incorporated many concepts of the paganism that it sought to eradicate or Christianize. Syncretism became a pragmatic and irresistible trend in the obligated assimilation of hundreds of pagan cultures. The evolving Roman-Germanic culture became inseparable to the culture of the Church. To become a Christian you had to become a Roman citizen culturally. Thus the Christianizing of a nation became the civilizing of a people.

As the fifth century came to a close it had been 16 generations since the Ascension. Barrnett and Johnson[16] estimate that the world is 19.9% Christians and 31.2% evangelized. The Scriptures had been translated into 13 languages. The total martyrs since AD 33 are estimated at 2,102,00[17], that is 0.8% of all Christians since the Church began, which translates into 5,600 per year.

---

[15] John W. Kennedy, *The Torch of the Testimony*, page 107
[16] David B. Barrett, and Todd M. Johnson, World Christian Trends AD 30- AD 2200: Interpreting the annual Christian megacensus.
[17] ED: This number is in error. 5,600 times 2000 years is 11,200,200 people.

Much of the knowledge of the Scriptures and the biblical basis of faith were lost in the pomp and ceremony of cultural and traditional religion, not to mention the intrigue and power manipulations to keep and expand the church's authority in a morally decaying world power struggle. There was no emperor in the West, the army was drafting every available man to battle the invading marauding tribal raiding armies, which forced people out of the urban cities into an isolated rural existence.[18]

We see this trend towards conflating faith and culture, a process that most often results in the people professing faith in Christ being conformed to the culture.

As the hand of providence moved to bring light to a people, He also moved to bring darkness to a people, just as He did in the centuries before John came crying in the wilderness. Power hungry men, bent on world domination, wrapped in religious clothes, spun a web of doctrine that was (as Andrew Miller put it) fit only for an ignorant and superstitious people. The Dark Ages was fit for this, as we read:

> The Dark Ages (5th to 15th centuries C.E.), was a time when the Church had the Bible locked up in the Latin language, and scholarship and learning were nearly nonexistent. However, with the birth of the Morning Star of the Reformation, John Wycliffe (1328-1384), and more officially in the 16th-century Reformation, and the

---

[18] Don Fanning, https://digitalcommons.liberty.edu/cgm_hist/3/

31

invention of the printing press in 1455, the restraints were loosened, and there was a rebirth of interest in the Greek language. Moreover, with the fall of Constantinople to the Turks 1453 C. E., many Greek scholars and their manuscripts were scattered abroad, resulting in a revival of Greek in the Western citadels of learning.[19]

The "church" that had locked up Scriptures in Latin was, of course, the papist cult. This religion held that common folk could not be trusted to read the Bible, but must implicitly trust certain men who had fought and clamored and swindled their way into positions of power. They made extensive use of images and statues which are, by nature, ambiguous in meaning - needing an educated, trusted person to explain the true meaning. The papist religion, indeed, is fit for ignorant and superstitious people. Andrew Miller also observed, "The church, we must remember, is an outcalling (Acts 15: 14) — called out from Jew and Gentile to witness that she was not of this world, but of heaven — that she is united to a glorified Christ, and not of this world, even as He is not of this world."[20]

In looking at the history of the church during the above period, we shall see in what the darkness consisted, and also that God had, here and there,

---

[19] Edward D. Andrews, Christian Publishing House Blog, https://christianpublishinghouse.co/2017/03/09/the-reign-of-the-king-james-version/amp/
[20] Miller, 169. See also Appendix 2 in this book.

His light-bearers who spread abroad the light of
the gospel of God as far as in them lay.[21]

This is what I hope to make clear: no matter the darkness
that this world and its system, run by wicked men can
bring, God always preserves a people for Himself, to
keep the light burning and shining bright - for His glory
and the good of His own. And He often uses those who
are at enmity with Him, as when He used Syria to punish
national Israel. In the Dark Ages, He used monks in the
Romish monastic system to make copies of Scripture -
so His Word would be preserved and His people not left
without a lamp.

*For You will light my lamp; The LORD my God will
enlighten my darkness. For by You I can run against a
troop, By my God I can leap over a wall. As for God,
His way is perfect; The word of the LORD is proven; He
is a shield to all who trust in Him.* (Psalm 18:28-30)

---

[21] George Morrish, *Darkness of the Dark Ages*, Introduction

In Darkness – Light!

3. Flickering Candles in Monasteries

I will lead the blind by a way they did not know; I will guide them on paths they have not known. I will turn darkness to light in front of them and rough places into level ground. This is what I will do for them, and I will not forsake them. (Isaiah 24:16)

No matter the acts of men, the Lord will provide for His people. By His Spirit, the light of the Word will be sufficient in our darkness hour.

"God hath never left himself without witness; but from time to time he raises up instruments to publish his grace, enriching them with gifts necessary for the edification of his Church, giving them his Spirit for their guide, and his truth for their rule; whereby they may distinguish the Church begun in Abel, from that which commenced in Cain. He also teaches them to define the Church by faith, and faith by the Holy Scripture."[1]

While we who are known by God should always trust His hand of providence, we cannot be ignorant of danger posed by the influence of cultural religion. Since the time of Paul the apostle there have been professing Christians who thought self-denial, asceticism, was the way to spiritual life (Col. 2:18). John of Antioch was caught up in the early monk culture fostered by the growing papist religion. In his review of the development of the papist system of monkery, Shelley rightly observed, "Temptations of the outer world were replaced by temptations of the inner world."[2]

---

[1] Jean Paul Perrin, *History Of The Ancient Christians*, page 27
[2] Shelley, 127

Yet God has not left us without a witness, a rock of truth that will not succumb to the siren call of the culture. Righteous Lot (2 Peter 2:7) did not seek out the covenant people of God when his city was destroyed and his wife died. He pleaded for another city of wickedness (Zoar) to be his home and then fled from there to the countryside, but not to where his uncle Abraham lived. Lot took his daughters to a cave, where the violence and sin of Zoar could not reach him. But Genesis 19:30-38 reveals the problem with isolation: your sin goes with you; you cannot hide from your sin by disciplining or punishing your body and mind. There is one refuge from sin, only One and we must never take our focus off Christ.

We can learn from Lot that isolation is not the way to holiness, yet countless men and women have been led astray into thinking isolation and asceticism are the way to holiness. On this foundation of sand, the institution of papist monasticism was built.

> By taking in the whole population of the Roman empire the church became, indeed, a church of the masses, a church of the people, but at the same time more or less a church of the world. Christianity became a matter of fashion. The number of hypocrites and formal professors rapidly increased; strict discipline, zeal, self-sacrifice, and brotherly love proportionally ebbed away; and many heathen customs and usages, under altered names, crept into the worship of God and the life of the Christian people. The Roman state had grown up under the

influence of idolatry, and was not to be magically transformed at a stroke. With the secularizing process, therefore, a paganizing tendency went hand in hand.[3]

Pagan worship of images was resisted by the infant Roman church, which had already begun veneration of relics. When Justinian emerged as emperor of what was left of the Roman empire in A.D. 525, he outlawed paganism; images of Christ and the martyrs soon appeared on the walls of the church buildings. At first, there seems to have been no evidence that worship was given to these, but, as Cunningham relates, the process of corruption of religion begins small but advances rapidly and widely, bringing image worship to the eastern church and image and statue worship into the western church. The second Council of Nice, also referred to as the Council of Trent, in 787, established the practice of image worship as the rule in the Roman church.

Leaders who appeared to understand the dangers of idolatry tied to these practices were opposed by monks, ascetics, and an uneducated people. John of Damascus was a major advocate of icons, basing his argument on "Plato's notion that everything we sense in this world is really an imitation of the eternal, original "form," which can be known only by the soul in the nonmaterial world. To deny, as the iconoclasts did, that any true icon could depict Christ, was, in effect, to deny the possibility of the Incarnation."[4]

---

[3] Schaff, 109
[4] Shelley, 158

Due to Constantine's work, "The line between church and world, between regenerate and unregenerate, between those who were Christians in name and those who were Christians in heart, was more or less obliterated, and in place of the former hostility between the two parties there came a fusion of them in the same outward communion of baptism and confession. This brought the conflict between light and darkness, truth and falsehood, Christ and antichrist, into the bosom of Christendom itself."[5] And yet, one light that was kept flickering within the emerging papist cult would greatly benefit believers in the coming generations. By the early 6th century, many monasteries had taken up the role of preserving and copying ancient texts, including Scripture. "Thus that very mode of life, which in its founder, Anthony, despised all learning, became in the course of its development an asylum of culture in the rough and stormy times of the migration and the crusades, and a conservator of the literary treasures of antiquity for the use of modern times."[6]

One region that was prioritized by the Roman monasterial activity was Ireland, a remote island that was neglected by many. Some say the monasteries in Ireland are responsible for the preservation of the world of Latin culture, through the work of securing these books from the crumbling culture in mainland Europe. As they went in search of books to save, they took their message into the land which was being ravaged by war.

Throughout mainland Europe invading barbarian tribes swept across Europe destroying

[5] Shelley, 109-110
[6] Ibid, 196

monasteries, towns, and any leadership. Europe was plunging into chaos. Beginning in 510 the Irish Peregrini [Irish Pilgrims], who were an unorganized wandering groups of hermits and preachers who had been trained in Irish monasteries, began to migrate across Europe and would do so for the next 300 years.

However, they were spreading a Celtic Christianity, which was independent of the Roman Catholic Church and all of its power structure. The Celtic Christianity had to be transformed to submission to Rome.

By 545 the Irish monasteries at Clonard has 3,000 monks and at Belfast over 3,000. For a considerable time these missionaries were sent back to the mainland to evangelize the unreached tribal groups and areas devastated by the plagues and marauding wars of barbarian conquests.

Clifton Warner of Regent College writes, "Celtic Christians knew of no other way of being a Christian but to be a Christian living in community. Peregrini were sent from a community, with others, to form the nucleus of a new community"[7]. Their lifestyle was four-fold[8]: (1) robust, with a great love for life and creation; (2) ascetic, because they voluntarily deprived themselves of many comforts for the love of God; reflective, giving serious attention to reading,

---

[7] Clifton D. S. Warner, "Celtic community, spirituality and mission." *Global Missiology for the 21st Century*, page 493
[8] J. T. McNeill, *Early Celtic Christianity*, page 157

study and the development of the mind (music, art, and worthy books); (4) contemplative, practicing solitude and prayerful meditation.[9]

By the 7th century, the Roman church had established itself as the religious and political power to be reckoned with in central Europe. All professing Christians who did not bow the knee to the pope were considered schismatics and heretics. "An inevitable consequence of the union of church and state was restriction of religious freedom in faith and worship, and the civil punishment of departure from the doctrine and discipline of the established church. ... All they say against the persecution of Christians by the heathen applies in full to the persecution of heretics by the church."[10]

There arose an uprising among the French monks in a small monastery at Cluny; they sought to purify the church from her secular and political interests, returning the church to her spiritual role. They were particularly fierce in their fight against Simony (the buying and selling of church offices), which was widespread through the papal empire. Duncan observes that "virtually the whole period from the eleventh century on was dominated by this mighty conflict."[11]

> Papal monachism demands entire renunciation, not only of sin, but also of property and of marriage, which are lawful in themselves, ordained by God himself, and indispensable to the continuance and welfare of the human race.

---

[9] Fanning, https://digitalcommons.liberty.edu/cgm_hist/3/
[10] Shelley, 122
[11] Duncan, 52-53

The poverty of the individual, however, does not exclude the possession of common property; and it is well known, that some monastic orders, especially the Benedictines, have in course of time grown very rich. The coenobite[12] institution requires also absolute obedience to the will of the superior, as the visible representative of Christ. As obedience to orders and sacrifice of self is the first duty of the soldier, and the condition of military success and renown, so also in this spiritual army in its war against the flesh, the world, and the devil, monks are not allowed to have a will of their own. ... Voluntary poverty, voluntary celibacy, and absolute obedience form the three monastic vows, as they are called, and are supposed to constitute a higher virtue and to secure a higher reward in heaven.[13]

Yet in the midst of the spiritual darkness spread by the papist cult as it consumed that cult, God had His own people (see chapter 5), as well as the use of various members of the popish religion, serving Him as they copied Scripture and preached from it, ensuring the Word would not be lost in the sea of depravity and darkness.

Jean Perrin captured testimony given to the piety, probity, and learning of the Waldenses, by their adversaries:

---

[12] the monastic tradition that emphases regulated community life, that is, in which the monks live together under a set of rules established by the ruling abbot.
https://orthodoxwiki.org/Cenobitic
[13] Schaff, 138-139

Claude de Seissel, Archbishop of Turin, renders this testimony touching the Waldenses: "As to their life and manners they are perfect, and irreprehensible, without reproach among men, addicting themselves with all their might to observe the commandments of God." Cardinal Baronius styles the Waldenses of Thoulouse good men, and peaceable persons, although elsewhere he falsely lays very many crimes to their charge.

As to their learning, Reinerius said, that they taught their children and their families the epistles and gospels. Jacobus de Riberia said, that they were so well instructed in the Holy Scriptures, that he had seen peasants who could recite the book of Job, verbatim; and several others who could perfectly repeat all the New Testament.[14]

The Lord Jesus told us, *"If the world hates you, understand that it hated Me before it hated you."* (John 15:18) Peter advised us, *"Dear friends, don't be surprised when the fiery ordeal comes among you to test you as if something unusual were happening to you. Instead, rejoice as you share in the sufferings of the Messiah, so that you may also rejoice with great joy at the revelation of His glory. If you are ridiculed for the name of Christ, you are blessed, because the Spirit of glory and of God rests on you. None of you, however, should suffer as a murderer, a thief, an evildoer, or a*

---

[14] Perrin, 43

meddler. But if anyone suffers as a "Christian," he should not be ashamed but should glorify God in having that name." (1 Peter 4:12-16) We should not be surprised that the Medieval world hated the children of God; we should not be surprised if our world hates us. It's naivety to think that we are the exception to what the Bible portrays as our lot. Some children of God that history recorded were treated horribly by professing Christians who could not tolerate anyone disagreeing with them.

> Bullinger speaks thus of the Waldenses: For four hundred years and more, in France, Italy, Germany, Poland, Bohemia, and other countries throughout the world, the Waldenses have made profession of the Gospel of Jesus, Christ, and have in several writings, and continual preachings, accused the pope as the true Antichrist, of whom the Apostle John foretold, and that therefore we ought to flee from him. These people, having undergone diverse and cruel torments, have constantly and openly given testimony to their faith by glorious martyrdoms, and still do the same to this day. Luther confessed that he hated the Waldenses, as persons consigned over to perdition, until having understood the piety of their faith by their confessions and writings, he perceived that those good men had been greatly wronged whom the pope had condemned as heretics, being rather worthy of the praise due to holy martyrs. Among the said Waldenses, he had found one thing worthy of admiration, and to be taken notice of as miraculous and unheard of in the popish

Church; that the said Waldenses, having forsaken all human doctrines, did meditate with all their power in the law of the Lord, day and night; that they were very expert in the Scriptures and well versed in them.[15]

John Kennedy's excellent book, *The Torch of The Testimony*, is an insightful look into the people God called out darkness and shone like lights in the wicked world in which they lived. "There were groups of believers who, among themselves owning only the name of 'Christians' or 'brethren', stood out strongly against the idolatry, sacramentalism, and other prevailing errors of the Catholic Church. They appear on the historical scene in the middle of the seventh century as 'Paulicians' in the region of Mesopotamia. ... The Catholic Church ascribed to them all sorts of erroneous doctrines. ... Whatever opinions may be held about the Paulicians, it is generally conceded that they had a particular respect for the authority of the Bible, advocated a life of simplicity, were devout and earnest people, and bore strong witness against the unsavoury practices of the Catholic Church. Their enemies testified against them, but their lives testified of Christ."[16]

The Paulicians accepted no central authority to rule over the scattered assemblies. ... They did not draw up any code of conduct to which they had commonly to subscribe as a basis for unity. ... Their spiritual unity lay in the life which they

---

[15] Perrin, 45
[16] John W. Kennedy, *The Torch of the Testimony*, pages 109-110

had in Christ, a life which manifested itself in their daily walk and witness.[17]

Another group that did not bow the knee to the growing Roman religion sprung from the work of Peter of Bruys.

> Not much is known of the life of this teacher. ... he is found preaching in Southern France soon after the beginning of the twelfth century, where he labored for twenty years, and he was burned as a heretic in the year 1126. His doctrines are known to us chiefly through his bitter enemy and persecutor, Peter the Venerable, Abbot of Clugny, who wrote a book against the heresy of the Petrobrusians. With due allowance for the mistakes honestly made by this prelate, we may deduce approximately the teachings of this body. We find their fundamental principle to be the rejection of tradition and an appeal to Scripture as the sole authority in religion. The abbot complains in his treatise that these heretics will not yield to tradition or the authority of the church, but demand Scripture proof for everything; because it would have been easy for him to confute them by quoting any quantity of passages from the Fathers, only these obstinate heretics would have none of the Fathers.

> In the preface to his treatise, the abbot sums up the errors of the Petrobrusians under five heads.

---

[17] Kennedy, 111

1. The first error is their denial that children, before the age of understanding, can be saved by the baptism of Christ, or that another's faith avails those who cannot exercise faith.

2. It is superfluous to build temples, since the church of God does not consist in a multitude of stones joined together, but in the unity of the believers assembled.

3. The Petrobrusians command the sacred crosses to be broken in pieces and burned, because that form or instrument by which Christ was so dreadfully tortured, so cruelly slain, is not worthy of any adoration, or veneration or supplication.

4. The Petrobrusians denied sacramental grace, especially the doctrine of transubstantiation, the keystone of the sacramental system.

5. They deride sacrifices, prayers, alms, and other good works by the faithful living for the faithful dead, and say that these things cannot aid any of the dead even in the least.[18]

The witness of Rome reveals to us brethren we should be able to relate to. All who call themselves Baptist have fellowship with these souls who went by various names throughout the Dark Ages, clinging to Scripture and seeking to honor the Lord rather than take the easy road of submission to the state-church.

Within the Romish system, God would stir the souls of men and use them to bring light to darkened places.one such man was Bernard of Clairvaux, 1090-1153, a preacher of monergistic salvation. "Nobody will be

---

[18] Henry Clay Vedder, *A Short History of the Baptists*, pages 46-47

justified in His sight by works of the law. … Conscious of our deficiency, we shall cry to heaven and God will have mercy on us. And on that day we shall know that God has saved us, not by the righteous works that we ourselves have done, but according to His mercy. … Therefore my beginning is solely of grace, and I have nothing which I can attribute to myself in predestination or in calling"[19]

Busenitz went on to observe:

> … throughout the medieval period, a number of Latin commentators echoed the Pauline language of faith alone (*sola fide*) when commenting on justification in the book of Romans. Examples include Cassiodorus (ca. 485-583), Lanfranc of Bec (ca. 1003-1089), Bruno of Cologne (1032-1101), and Robert of Melun (ca. 1100 -1167). A survey of these medieval commentators suggests that they limited their understanding of justification primarily to the remission of past sins only. Nevertheless, it is significant to not that the Reformers were not the first ones to use the phrase *sola fide* in their interpretation of Romans.[20]

Historians help us see the monks who were deceived and coerced to live in that system were men, real human beings like you and me. Trapped by an evil system – which was the norm throughout much of human history

[19] Nathan Busenitz, *Long Before Luther*, page 137
[20] Ibid, 138

– yet used by God for His purposes. Just as Nebuchadnezzar was.

> Orthodox monks were living men; — there was blood in their veins, and there was bile too;— they had tongues, they took hold of pens, they made themselves listened to; —they knew how to deal with their enemies; and a great part of what is called church history, is nothing but the story of the contests between these very men, and their opponents. Very soon the profane multitude learned that it would henceforward be at their peril to speak slightingly of holy ascetics, and that, to make a jest of cowls, bare feet, beads, crucifixes, relics, and noon candles, was dangerous sport, and might end in being burned alive.[21]

A main source of comfort for God's people ought to be knowledge of providence. Providence refers to God working all things to fulfill His purposes. The word providence does not appear in the Bible; the concept of providence is writ large everywhere in Scripture. God's providence is an outworking of His sovereignty. If God is not sovereign - before all creation - He cannot work to design, order, and execute His decree in creation. If God were not sovereign, there would be no providence; the world would suffer through happenstance, chance, and luck.

There are two aspects of providence: The mundane: *The lot is cast into the lap, But **its every decision is from the***

---

[21] *Ancient Christianity, & the doctrines of the Oxford Tracts for the times*, Isaac Taylor, 1840, Dedicatory Letter

LORD (Proverbs 16:33). And the divine: *When the **time came to completion**, God sent His Son, born of a woman, born under the law, to redeem those under the law, so that we might receive adoption as sons.* (Galatians 4:4-5). Nothing is left to chance or happenstance; *every* "decision" of a die being cast is from YHWH. When the time was right, when all things had been made ready, God sent forth His Son, all for reasons that God has ordained to fulfill His purposes. Since He is good to His own, we can trust His hand of providence even when we don't understand it or don't see it. We can trust God if man slays us; that is the worse man can do. All who are in Christ are secure in His grip (John 10:27 - 30).

God does not leave us to a fatalistic view of our temporal lives nor does He lead us to think we should have our best life now. We live here, now, for the glory of God and the good of His people, knowing the life He has purchased is that of eternal life, which will be lived out on the new earth - where righteousness dwells. While we have breath, let us love one another in word and deed, fixing our eyes on the heavens. For man will always try to force men to submit to their vane traditions that distract us from Christ.

> About the year of our Lord 1160, it was made a capital crime for any person not to acknowledge, after the words of consecration were pronounced by the priest, that the body of our Lord Jesus Christ was actually present in the "Host," or Mass-wafer, under the accident of bread, with its roundness and whiteness — even that very same body, as large as it was when it hung upon the

cross; the bread vanishing, and being transubstantiated into the actual flesh of Christ. That doctrine was unknown to the Apostles, who never made mention of such a mystery; and was also unheard of by the primitive Churches, who never taught that an expiatory sacrifice was now to be made for the living and the dead.[22]

Peter Waldo is another child of God we should connect with. Historians are not sure of Peter Waldo's name, but there is wide consensus as to who he was and how God used him. Waldo was born in the mid-12th century and by 1170 had become a wealthy merchant in Lyon, France. Through the hand of providence, circumstances forced Waldo to take stock of his soul – he had no shield, no hiding place from the judge of all flesh.

The first thing he resolved was to read the Bible. But since it only existed in the Latin Vulgate, and his Latin was poor, he hired two scholars to translate it into the vernacular so he could study it.

Next, he sought spiritual counsel from a priest, who pointed him to the rich young ruler in the Gospels and quoted Jesus: "One thing you still lack. Sell all that you have and distribute to the poor, and you will have treasure in heaven; and come, follow me" (Luke 18:22). Jesus' words pierced Waldo's heart. Like the rich young ruler, Waldo suddenly realized he had been serving Mammon, not God. But unlike the rich young ruler who walked away from Jesus,

---

[22] Perrin, 27

Waldo repented and did exactly what Jesus said: he gave away all he had to the poor (after making adequate provision for his wife and daughters). From that point on, he determined to live in complete dependence on God for his provision.[23]

This translation was the first Bible given to Europe in a common tongue since the Latin Vulgate had been published. As he studied and preached the Bible, Waldo became more and more disgusted with the false teaching, ecclesiology, and practice from Rome. Preaching without sanction from Rome was forbidden; criticizing Rome was prohibited; and in 1185 Pope Lucius III excommunicated him. Waldo, like many others who saw the light of truth while being held captive by Rome, did not leave Rome, but sought to reform it. History teaches us this is, humanly speaking, a fool's errand.

The Archbishop of Lyons, John de Belseo Mayons, having been informed that Waldo made profession of teaching the people and that he boldly condemned the vices, luxury, and arrogance, of the popes and their clergy, inhibited him from teaching any more. The prelate declared, that Waldo was only a layman, and exceeded the bounds of his condition; and therefore that he should restrict himself within his prohibition, under pain of excommunication and of being proceeded against as a heretic. Waldo replied, that he could not be silent in a

[23] Jon Bloom, The First Tremor,
https://www.desiringgod.org/articles/the-first-tremor

matter of so great importance as was the salvation of men; and that he would rather obey God who enjoined to speak, than man who commanded him to be silent.[24]

Under Pope Innocent III, the cult of Rome enlisted the king of Hungary and, in 1203, cowed the Bosnian leaders, outlawing all the "heretics." "But great numbers of ordinary believers were not to be subjugated thus easily. They had found life in Christ, a satisfying rule in the Word of God, and had a faith in God which had not been dependent upon the conversion of their rulers. They refused to submit."[25] This persecution of God's people continued throughout the 14th and 15th centuries, culminating in the Turkish conquest of Bosnia in 1463, resulting in four centuries of Muslim rule. And under this rule, "the bright witness of the Friends of God in Bosnia seemed to die out."[26]

"The reaction of the Roman Church to the Waldenses and Cathars (or Albigenses, another name by which some groups of believers were known) came to a head in a far-reaching decision which was made at the Council of Toulouse in 1229."[27] This council recognized that "Scripture was the basis of the main opposition to the Church of Rome"[28] and they "determined to remove this mischievous reading matter from the hands of the laity, who were henceforth forbidden the use of the Bible apart from the Latin

---

[24] Perrin, 28
[25] Kennedy, 116
[26] Ibid, 117
[27] Ibid, 121
[28] Ibid

Psalter and such other portions as were contained in the breviary. It was furthermore decreed that no part of the Scriptures should be translated into the tongues of the common people. ... The fierce wrath provoked by the possession and reading of the Scriptures highlights for us the important place which the Word of God must occupy in the life of the local church."[29]

> The dispersion of Waldo and his disciples was the means which God made use of to spread the doctrine of Waldo almost throughout all Europe. Dubravius says, "Philip Augustas, King of France, pushed on by the Romish ecclesiastics, took up arms against the Waldenses of Piedmont, razed three hundred houses of the gentlemen who followed their party, and destroyed some walled towns. He also pursued them into Flanders whither they had fled, and caused a great number of them to be burned."[30]

Much of what ended up being formalized by the Council of Trent had its beginning in the rulings of the Council of Toulouse, which "systematized the procedure to be followed by the Inquisition."[31] While the cult of Rome raged against the people of God, God Himself protected His flock and gave them wisdom and grace to press on for their Savior. "The teaching of John Wycliffe in England and John Hus in Bohemia was exercising a powerful influence in those countries, and many

---

[29] Kennedy, 121
[30] Perrin, 29
[31] Kennedy, 121

believers sought freedom to worship God in these foreign lands."[32]

"Ludwig of Bavaria, supported by the Franciscan Spirituals, declared Pope John XXII (1316-1334) a "formal heretic" in the Reichstag at Nuremberg in 1323."[33] This brought retribution upon Germany: "Germany alone was under interdict for twenty years, which meant that no public religious service could be held, no sacrament could be publicly administered, no bell could sound."[34] That Rome forbade the ringing of bells reveals the superstitious nature of their religion. But it is difficult for us to imagine the hardship these papal interdicts imposed. The Roman Catholic Church was central to life in the Dark Ages, and to be denied access to religious life, the sacraments, and the approval of the priests was a serious punishment for those who had been seduced by the papacy.

"Even within the Roman Church there were voices raised to contend against its unwarranted use of authority and the flagrant evil practices which seemed to be the norm."[35] Marsilius of Padna was a rector in Paris when he, in 1324, published *Defensor Pacis*. This shined the light of truth on Rome's evil practice, showing "that the standard in faith and conduct is the Bible. The church is the company of those who trust in Christ, not the ecclesiastical organization with its Popes, Bishops, and clergy. The latter, therefore, have no

---

[32] Ibid
[33] Karl Adam, *Roots of the Reformation*, page 12
[34] Ibid
[35] Kennedy, 124

authority to define Christian truth and compel obedience to their decrees."[36]

John Wycliffe was considered one of the brightest scholars of his day. He taught in Oxford and used that platform to teach how Rome had banished the Word of God, urging those who claimed Christ to use it in their worship. "In 1374 Wycliffe became rector of Lutterworth and was preaching the Word to an ever-widening circle. The source of faith, he taught, is the Gospel of Jesus Christ. The Pope can claim no arbitrary authority, but must be subject to God through His Word as everyone else."[37] He was charged with heresy in 1377 but retained his freedom. He was determined to make the Bible available to English people in their common tongue. "Wycliffe was not conversant with Hebrew and Greek, but he was a good Latin scholar, and the translation, completed between 1382 and 1384 was from the Latin Vulgate."[38] Wycliffe published a tract in 1381 retracting his long attachment to Rome's heretical doctrine of transubstantiation, calling it a "blasphemous deceit, contrary to Scripture."[39]

Wycliffe remained a Roman Catholic until he died but argued against the papal view of salvation by works and its ecclesiastical construct of Bishops and Popes. He saw that Christ is the only head of His people. Wycliffe and those who saw things the same way were called Lollards, likely a term of derision meaning "babblers." "Their preaching was no mere condemnation of Rome,

---

[36] Ibid, 124 - 125
[37] Kennedy, 125
[38] Ibid
[39] Ibid

but the positive setting forth of the Gospel of grace which brought liberation and life."[40] This is a note every child of God should learn: exposing error cannot save anyone; only the Spirit-delivered gospel is given that role. Wycliffe died a natural death in 1384, under the protection King Edward III, who maintained England's king was not subordinate to the Pope.

> In Wycliffe's day the clergy were notoriously ignorant of Scripture, and not without cause, for the free access of the Bible to the common man would have spelt the ruin of the Roman system. Why was there such violent opposition to the translation of the Scripture into the vernacular language? One of the main reasons was the threat this would have posed to the Catholic ecclesiasticism. On the continent of Europe, for example, vernacular versions of the Bible were in use among the Waldenses and others, and wherever the authority of the Word was recognized, the Pope protested his own assumed authority in vain.[41]

"Through the marriage of Richard II of England to a Bohemian Princess, Anna, in 1383, new avenues of contact were opened up between Bohemia and England. ... Jerome came under the influence of Wycliffe's teaching and returned to his own country to preach the 'new' doctrines with great boldness."[42] Jan Hus was one Bohemian that was influenced by these 'new' doctrines and he began proclaiming the Gospel and denouncing

---

[40] Ibid, 126
[41] Kennedy, 127
[42] Ibid, 128

Rome with fiery eloquence. Hus was excommunicated and Wycliffe's papers branded as heresy and burned up. "Bohemia was in confusion. The Council of Constance which convened in 1414 was approaching, and the situation in Bohemia affected by the teaching of Wycliffe and Hus demanded its attention. Hus, invited to attend, was given a promise of safe conduct by the Emperor of the Holy Roman Empire, Sigismund. ... The council, meanwhile, received a very convenient 'revelation from the Holy Spirit' that the church is not bound by any promise made to a heretic. ... In 1415, after a service in which he was publicly and shamefully degraded, Jan Hus died a martyr's death, burnt at the stake. Jerome of Prague, the man through whom Hus had been brought to the light, was soon to follow the same way."[43]

It is said that Hus means "goose" in Bohemian. This ties in to a moment in history that would serve as a light for over a century. When Jan Hus was at the stake, he was asked to recant his teachings. His reply still echoes in the souls of the saints: "You are now going to burn a goose, but in a century, you will have a swan which you can neither roast nor boil." 102 years later, Frederick of Saxony had a dream about a monk who wrote on the church door of Wittenberg with a pen so large that it reached to Rome. The more those in authority tried to break the pen, the stronger it became. When asked how the pen got so strong, the monk replied "The pen belonged to an old goose of Bohemia, a hundred years old." The following day, Martin Luther posted his 95 Theses against indulgences on the door of the Castle

---

[43] Kennedy, 129

Church in Wittenberg. Luther was referred to as the Swan, recognizing the hand of providence in raising up the goose as one in a long line of men who would not be silent.

Teachers rose up as sweet gospel fruit, after the soil had been watered by the death of Hus and Jerome. Peter Cheltschizki was one who taught the church was a spiritual organism and "he sought that there should be a return to the simple practice of apostolic days where believers gathered together purely on the grounds of their fellowship with God and one another for carrying out their commission of representing Christ in the world. About the middle of the fifteenth century these various congregations were known as the Unitas Fratrum (united Brethren). They had no desire to form any new party of sect, for they recognized their complete oneness of spirit with Christian brethren in every country where they might be found. They did, however, declare themselves to be separated from the Church of Rome. ... Down through the ages God has prepared a remnant through which a testimony to Him has been maintained and His purposes worked out."[44]

Henry Clay Vedder was a New England Baptist historian from the late 19th and early 20th centuries. He wrote a short book showing how records kept by the papist cult show what the people of God, the Waldenses, were up to. "None of our testimony comes directly from the Waldenses. Our witnesses are all Roman Catholics, men of learning and ability, but as deeply prejudiced against a heretic as men could possibly be. This establishes at the outset a presumption against the

---

[44] Kennedy, 130

trustworthiness of their testimony, and is a warning to us that we must weigh it most carefully, and scrutinize every detail before receiving it."[45] Some of the sources for his data were Roman inquisitors, skilled at coercing information from people.

He builds on the credibility of his work by establishing the close proximity in time between the events cited and the reports he found. "The documents from which quotations will be made, with few exceptions, are believed by the most competent scholars to have been composed by the year 1250 A. D., several of them before the year 1225. As the beginning of the events related by them cannot be placed earlier than the year 1170, it is evident that we have in this case as nearly contemporary accounts as could well be expected."[46]

One of the earliest mentions of the Waldenses was found in a decree of Pope Lucius III., issued in 1181: "We decree to put under a perpetual anathema the Cathari and Patarini and those who falsely call themselves Humiliati or Poor of Lyons, the Passaging Josephini, Arnaldistae." [47] Vedder says there is no doubt that the name "Poor of Lyons" is intended to describe those heretics known to us as Waldenses, since this was one of the earliest and most common names of the sect.

---

[45] Henry Clay Vedder, *Origin and Early Teachings of the Waldenses, according to Roman Catholic Writers of the Thirteenth Century*, epub location 4%
[46] Ibid, epub location 7%
[47] Vedder, *Origin and Early Teachings of the Waldenses, according to Roman Catholic Writers of the Thirteenth Century*, epub location 7%

In 1194, Alphonso, king of Aragon, issued this decree: "We command that the Waldenses or Insabati, who call themselves by another name, Poor of Lyons, and all other heretics, of whom there is no number, anathematized by the holy church, to depart and flee from our entire kingdom and domain, as enemies of the cross of Christ, violators of the Christian religion, public enemies of ourselves and of the kingdom. If anyone therefore, from this day forth, shall presume to receive into his house the aforesaid Waldenses and other heretics, of whatever profession they may be, or to listen to their deadly preaching in any place, or to give them food, or any other aid, let him know that he will incur the wrath of Almighty God and ours; and his goods shall be confiscated without remedy of appeal, and he shall be punished just as for the crime of treason."[48]

Stephen de Bourbon, also known as Stephen de bella villa, was a member of the Dominican order. "He spent much of his life in the very region where the Waldenses had their origin, personally knew many of the chief actors, and died at Lyons in 1261. Part of his materials were thus gathered at first hand; the rest he obtained as an inquisitor — "as I know and have found out by many inquisitions and confessions of theirs under trial," he tells us, "as well of the perfect as of the believers, written down from their mouths and received from many witnesses against them.""[49]

---

[48] Vedder, *Origin and Early Teachings of the Waldenses, according to Roman Catholic Writers of the Thirteenth Century*, epub location 10%
[49] Ibid, epub location 17%

Speaking of the Roman Catholic Church, Vedder reported, "When the church saw them usurp the office of preaching, which had not been committed to them, since they were uneducated and laymen, she prohibited them, as was fitting, and excommunicated them when unwilling to obey. But they despised in this the keys of the church, saying that the clergy did this through envy, because they saw them (Waldenses) to be better than themselves, and to teach better, and in consequence of this to have greater favor with the people. For a good and perfect work, such as teaching the faith and doctrine of Christ, no one should or can be excommunicated, and against the doctrine of Christ no one ought by any means to obey anyone prohibiting such a good work."[50]

As with others whom God called out of the darkness of the Romish religion, in his early days, "Waldo had no idea that he was a heretic, and no intention of causing a schism. He was not guilty of any offense in having the Scriptures translated or in repeating and explaining them to others. It was not until the synod of Toulouse, in 1229, that the Roman church, taught by its experience with the Waldenses the danger of letting the common people have the Scriptures in the vernacular, forbade laymen to have either the Old or the New Testament, save such portions as might be contained in the ordinary books of devotion. The synod of Tarragon, 1234, followed up this prohibition by forbidding even priests to have the Scriptures in the vernacular and

---

[50] Vedder, *Origin and Early Teachings of the Waldenses, according to Roman Catholic Writers of the Thirteenth Century*, epub location 38%

commanding all who owned copies to bring them to their bishop to be burned."[51]

Of the Waldenses, the cult of Rome described them as those who:

1. Hold to the doctrine of Christ and His apostles, without the decrees of the church.
2. Deny purgatory, claiming God alone absolves from sin and that a saved person is with the Lord immediately after the first death.
3. Deny efficacious prayers for the dead or by the dead.
4. Deny indulgences.
5. Deny that the Roman Catholic Church is of Christ, saying it is rather the harlot of Babylon.
6. Deny the feast of candles, adoration of the cross and other religious rites not found in Scripture.
7. Deny the mass and transubstantiation. "Neither the body of Christ, nor any other creature, such as images and crosses, is to be adored and worshiped with any sort of adoration, without idolatry." (Disputatio inter Catholicum et Paterinum Haereticum, Martene and Durand, Vol. V, pp. 1727 f.)
8. Claim the Scriptures in a common tongue have as much authority as in Latin.[52]

By the things they deny, as documented by their enemy, the people known as Waldenses demonstrate themselves to be brothers and sisters to all who rightly

---

[51] Ibid, epub location 48%

[52] Vedder, *Origin and Early Teachings of the Waldenses, according to Roman Catholic Writers of the Thirteenth Century*, taken from narrative in epub locations 66 – 79%

profess Christ Jesus as Savior and Lord. The record of these saints ought to encourage us, much in the same way Hebrews 11 does.

The Waldenses "say that a man is then truly for the first time baptized, when he is brought into their heresy. But some say that baptism does not profit little children because they are not yet able to believe. (David of Augsburg.)"[53] "If he does not repent, baptism does not profit him; if he repents, he is already justified, and all his sin is remitted. Therefore baptism has no power of remitting sin for him, and water baptism is not at all necessary for remission of sins of others said baptism does not avail without imposition of hands. (Alanus.)"[54]

Edward Andrews helps us see another aspect of God using people in the midst of His enemy, near the end of the Dark Ages:

> About fifty years later, or at the beginning of the sixteenth century, Ximenes, archbishop of Toledo, Spain, a man of rare capability and honor, invited foremost scholars of his land to his university at Alcala to produce a multiple-language Bible—not for the common people, but for the educated. The outcome would be the Polyglot, named Complutensian corresponding to the Latin of Alcala. This would be a Bible of six large volumes, beautifully bound, containing the Old Testament in four languages (Hebrew, Aramaic, Greek, and Latin) and the New

---

[53] Vedder, *Origin and Early Teachings of the Waldenses, according to Roman Catholic Writers of the Thirteenth Century*, epub location 79%
[54] Ibid, epub location 83%

Testament in two (Greek and Latin). For the Greek New Testament, these scholars had only a few manuscripts available to them, and those of late origin. One may wonder why this was the case when they were supposed to have access to the Vatican library. This Bible was completed in 1514, providing the first printed Greek New Testament, but did not receive approval by the pope to be published until 1520 and was not released to the public until 1522.[55]

While some were determined to keep the Scriptures away from common folk, others worked tirelessly to get the Word of God into the hands of the common man. Why would men give up wealth and position to fight for the Truth? We read of the liberation that comes when a man is born by the Spirit and begins to understand the Bible. This is what causes men and women to forsake the world and pursue their Savior.

> The clearness of the Holy Scriptures struck each reader. None of the systematic or aphoristic forms of the school were to be found there: it was the language of human life which they discovered in the divine writings. ... Above all, the life of our Savior, so divine and so human, had an inexpressible charm which captivated the simple. ... This fall and this restoration......they are mine. That old death and this new life.....I have passed through them. That flesh and that

---

[55] Edward D. Andrews, Christian Publishing House Blog, https://christianpublishinghouse.co/2017/03/09/the-reign-of-the-king-james-version/amp/ (accessed 31 August 2022.)

spirit.....I know them. This law and this grace, the faith, these works, this slavery, this glory, this Christ and the Belial.....all are familiar to me. It is my own history that I find in this book.[56]

This is why we can have confidence that, no matter how dark the times may be, God's hand is holding up and guiding and protecting His people so they will shine like lights in the darkness of this present age.

But you are a chosen race, a royal priesthood, a holy nation, a people for His possession, so that you may proclaim the praises of the One who called you out of darkness into His marvelous light. (1 Peter 2:9)

---

[56] J.H. Merle D'Aubigne, *History of the Reformation*, Volume Five, Book XIX, pages 266-267

In Darkness – Light!

4. False Religion

*Because of our God's merciful compassion, the Dawn
from on high will visit us to shine on those who live in
darkness and the shadow of death, to guide our feet into
the way of peace.* (Luke 1:78-79)

The means of peace in a storm is trust in God, in His
character and His care for His people. Because of His
mercy, He will provide light enough for us to walk on
the pathway of peace in our dark world.

> The early church considered itself a body, a
> living organism, a new people, completely
> incompatible with any other people or any
> natural community. ... In official Byzantine
> doctrine, however, the state was compared to a
> body not in this early Christian sense, nor
> because all the subjects of the empire had become
> genuine church members. The figure of the
> imperial body arose from pagan thinking. The
> state itself was concerned as a community
> established by God, and it embraced the whole
> life of a man. The visible representative of God
> within it, who performed his will and dispensed
> his blessings, was the emperor.[1]

While the Roman Catholic monasteries were used of
God for the preservation of Scripture, they were largely
the source of much mischief, abuse, false teaching and
bizarre behavior. There is a long-standing belief in the
papist cult that His people *"fill up the suffering of*

---

[1] Shelley, 156

67

Christ" (Colossians 1:24) by intentionally causing suffering in their person. Some flagellate themselves in various ways,[2] others combined extreme self-discipline with isolation.

> In the fifth century a new and quite original path was broken by Symeon, the father of the Stylites or pillar saints, who spent long years, day and night, summer and winter, rain and sunshine, frost and heat, standing on high, unsheltered pillars, in prayer and penances, and made the way to heaven for themselves so passing hard, that one knows not whether to wonder at their unexampled self-denial, or to pity their ignorance of the gospel salvation. On this giddy height the anchoretic asceticism reached its completion. ... Symeon invented, in 423, a new sort of holiness, and lived, some two days' journey (forty miles) east of Antioch, for six and thirty years, until his death, upon a pillar, which at the last was nearly forty cubits high; for the pillar was raised in proportion as he approached heaven and perfection.
>
> There St. Symeon stood many long and weary days, and weeks, and months, and years, exposed to the scorching sun, the drenching rain, the crackling frost, the howling storm, living a life of daily death and martyrdom, groaning under the load of sin, never attaining to the true comfort and peace of soul which is derived from a child-like trust in Christ's infinite merits, earnestly striving after a superhuman holiness, and looking

---

[2] http://news.bbc.co.uk/2/hi/uk_news/magazine/8375174.stm

to a glorious reward in heaven, and immortal fame on earth.[3]

A more biblical view of Colossians 1:24 would be that the "lack is the gap of sufferings between the present reach of the gospel and the suffering necessary to establish a gospel presence among all the Gentiles, paralleling Jesus's own mission to bring the gospel to the Jewish people. ... Paul's sufferings have benefited both the Gentiles broadly (as seen in the expansive reach of the message, Col. 1:6a) and the Colossian church specifically (as seen in their adherence to the gospel, Col. 1:6b–8)."[4] The sufferings of Christ as regards the payment for the sins of His people cannot be added to or improved upon by sinful people, as the Romish religion teaches: "Suffering for the sake of the Body is meritorious. It is a good deed that is rewarded by grace, and all such deeds serve to build up the Body of Christ."[5] The bottom-line difference between biblical Christianity and the Romish counterfeit is justification. The Bible teaches that salvation is by grace, through faith in Christ; saved not by good works we do but saved to do good works. Rome teaches that salvation is by faith in Christ which is improved and supplemented by "good" works.

But Rome was not alone in teaching heresy. From about 662 Islam became a militant faith, "with its gospel being spread not only by word of mouth but by the sword. ... By the early part of the eighth century it was threatening

---

[3] Schaff, 166-167

[4] https://www.thegospelcoalition.org/article/lacking-in-christs-afflictions/

[5] https://catholicstand.com/complete-suffering-of-christ/

to overrun western Europe itself, having penetrated as far as central France. … Under the leadership of Charles Martel, they [the Franks] decisively defeated the Mohommedans in 732 in a battle near the present French cities of Tours and Poiters. This was one of the decisive battles of world history, for it marked the turning point in the struggle between Islam and Christianity."[6]

Islam served Rome as means to garner support, as popes and bishops used the Muslim advances to stir up fear in the people of Europe, holding out protection by the papacy as God's own means of protection. But Rome always has Rome as its main benefactor.

> In A.D. 527, Justinian became emperor. He was a moral man, and took much interest in all ecclesiastical questions. … He spent an enormous sum of money on the re-building of the church of St. Sophia at Constantinople, which had been burnt down at the time when Chrysostom was banished, and once after. When the emperor viewed the beautiful building at its dedication (A.D. 544) he thanked God for having permitted him to complete so great a work; but then impiously exclaimed, "O Solomon, I have surpassed thee!" Three years after an earthquake shattered the dome of the church; but Justinian rebuilt it with still increased height and splendour.
>
> To this cathedral were attached, by one of its laws, sixty priests, a hundred deacons, forty

---

[6] Duncan, 44-45

70

deaconesses, ninety subdeacons, a hundred and
ten readers, five and twenty singers, and a
hundred door-keepers. Alas! how the simplicity
of the early worship in the church had become
destroyed![7]

As the papacy accumulated power and influence, more
people and nations were brought under her dominion.
Gregory I, styled as Gregory the Great, lived when the
darkness of the Dark Ages was beginning. In fighting
off the Lombards in Italy, Gregory the Great played a
major role, establishing the infant papacy with political
gravitas that lasted for centuries. "After Gregory, the
pope was no longer only a Christian leader; he was also
an important political figure in European politics: God's
Consul. ... while Gregory protested high-sounding titles,
he claimed and exercised, as far as he had the
opportunity and power, the oversight over the whole
church of Christ."[8]

He had long desired to take what he perceived as the
Christian message to England, and when he was pope,
he sent the head of his monastery, Augustine (not the
same Augustine who was, 200 years prior, Bishop of
Hippo), to do the job in the late 6th century. Augustine
was then made archbishop of Canterbury, having
convinced the king Ethelbert of Kent, of the Christian
religion as defined by Rome. "Gregory had counselled
that the heathen temples should not be destroyed, but
consecrated for worship, so that the people might be the
more easily induced to attend. Festivals also were held
at the ancient times, booths erected, animals slain, and

---

[7] Morrish, chapter 2
[8] Shelley, 177

the people fed — but consecrated to some saint. Their heathen habits would thus not be so much violated as if all were swept away at once. The new religion, indeed, was to be accommodated to heathen customs! And this was called Christianity!"[9]

Gregory developed seven doctrines that set the papist religion apart from biblical Christianity:

> 1. Doctrine of man: "Gregory stressed that Adam's fall affected all his descendants, weakening but not destroying their freedom of will. Thus once man has been moved by grace, he may cooperate with it and win merit for himself by his good works, which are the joint product of divine grace and human will."

> 2. Water baptism: "In baptism, God grants forgiving grace freely without any merit on man's part, but for sins committed after baptism man must make atonement by penance, which is simply a form of punishment inflicted by the man himself instead of by God."

> 3. Works of man: "The meritorious works, without which penance is not complete, are deeds involving sacrifice or suffering, such as almsgiving, ascetic practices, and prayers at all hours of the day. The greater our sins the more we must do to make up for them, and the more careful we must be to avoid them in the future. Whether we have done enough to atone for them we cannot know until after death."

---

[9] Morrish, chapter 4

4. The help of the saints. Gregory is quoted: "Our holy martyrs are ready to be your advocates, they desire to be asked, indeed if I may say so, they entreat that they may be entreated. Seek them as helpers of your prayer; turn to them that they may protect you in your guilt."

5. Holy Relics: "Gregory encouraged the collection and veneration of holy remains of the saint and martyrs locks of hair, fingernails, toes, pieces of clothing. Gregory taught - and most of his contemporaries believed - that these items possessed great powers, including that of self-defense."

6. Purgatory: The place where "sins could still be atoned." A "place of purification and suffering, not for those who die with serious offenses still charged against them, but for those who are not as yet altogether righteous. At death the perfectly holy go at once to heaven and the wicked to hell, while those of an intermediate character, who still have minor sins for which penance must be done, spend a season in purgatory."

7. The Holy Eucharist: "the supreme miracle, the key to all other expressions of divine power." The "Eucharist is a communion with Christ whose body and blood are really present in the bread and wine."[10]

Gregory also published "*Dictatus Papae*, in which he claimed for the Pope the right to depose unworthy

---

[10] Shelley, 179-80

princes and release their subjects from their oaths of allegiance, inspired papal policy all through the Middle Ages. This certainly added a corrosive bitterness and a devastating violence"[11] which lasted for centuries.

From the sixth century onward, the emerging Roman Catholic Church and the imperial government both encouraged the development of Christian icon-making and the honoring of monastic holy men. They did not realize that the uncontrolled multiplying of icons and holy men would incline people to confine their Christian devotion to local shrines and figures, reducing the influence of the papacy. Such is fallen man's tendency to attach divinity to places and things that can be seen and touched.

> The practice of the Catholic Church in adding to her worship things unheard-of in the New Testament and in the early Churches reaches an astounding degree when we note the multiplicity of ceremonies, rituals, vestments, genuflections, signs of the cross, and the multitude of things referred to above. Where did all these things come from? It is readily acknowledged by eminent Catholic writers that many of these customs, rites, paraphernalia, and practices were taken from Roman and Greek paganism, the Jewish Old Testament ritualism, and pagan religions, such as Buddhism, Mohammedanism, etc. Gregory I, Bishop of Rome, advised the use of heathen rites in order to attract them to the Church. Cardinal Newman acknowledged that many of the "Sacramentals" are of pagan origin.

---

[11] Adams, 11

Among the number he mentions are Incense, Candles, Holy Water, Tonsure, Vestments, Images, and several others.[12]

It seems the "seeker sensitive" doctrine is older than Rick Warren, but from a source no better than evangelicalism's king of pragmatism. It does explain why Warren has long been a friend to Rome. Wendell Rone's reference to Cardinal Newman is substantiated:

> The use of temples, and these dedicated to particular saints, and ornamented on occasions with branches of trees; incense, lamps, and candles; votive offerings on recovery from illness; holy water; asylums; holydays and seasons, use of calendars, processions, blessings on the fields; sacerdotal vestments, the tonsure, the ring in marriage, turning to the East, images at a later date, perhaps the ecclesiastical chant, and the Kyrie Eleison[13], are all of pagan origin, and sanctified by their adoption into the Church.[14]

The arrogance of the papacy is in clear view. Nadab and Abihu were struck dead for using their own judgment to determine the content of the offering of incense to YHWH, He burned them with fire and forbade Aaron to

---

[12] Wendell Rone, *The Baptist Faith and Roman Catholicism*, page 234

[13] A Latin transliteration of a Greek phrase meaning "Lord have mercy!" Used as a chant in Roman Catholic liturgy.
https://www.catholic.com/encyclopedia/Kyrie-Eleison

[14] John Henry Newman, *An Essay on the Development of Christian Doctrine*, pages 359 - 360

make a display of mourning for his sons.[15] Yet the papist religion can "sanctify" all sorts of admittedly pagan practices, making them acceptable in the sight of God and mandatory practice within "the church." This encourages neglect of Scripture and of God, as man has become the judge of what pleases Him.

We have boldness to approach God because of our union with Christ. We as mere men have no basis to think we can make something acceptable to God; thinking this way reveals we have swallowed the serpent's temptation and put ourselves in the place of God, determining what is good and what is evil. This should not be so!

Some ordinary "Christians may fail to distinguish between the holy objects or holy person and the spiritual reality it stood for and fall into idolatry."[16] Shelley appears to be accepting of the "proper use" of these unbiblical practices and sees a distinction between "ordinary Christians" and their leaders. Men who want to manipulate others use ambiguous symbols (icons or art) which must be interpreted by the "leaders" for the "ordinary Christians." Is it possible that those "ordinary Christians" who are so easily led astray are no Christians at all, but subjects of the state-church only?

Those who follow false religion are ever vulnerable to the allures of the world – lust of the eyes, lust of the flesh, and pride of life. "The church in England became rich, by kings and wealthy persons making over to the church their property, to insure the favour of heaven.

---

[15] Leviticus 10:1 – 7.
[16] Shelley, 157

Corruption rapidly followed, and monasteries and nunneries became the seats of debauchery. In the council of Cloveshoo, in 747, it was ordered that monasteries should not be turned into places of amusement "for harpers and buffoons." It is recorded that many nobles became abbots, that they might lead easy and jolly lives with companions like themselves."[17]

In describing the papist fight against the barbarians who had overrun much of Europe, Shelley tells the story of Boniface of the eighth century. Boniface had determined to chop down the large oak tree that served as the cultic center of the "forest of Thor" in Germany. As he stuck the tree with his ax, the story goes, God blew the tree over. "The pagans marveled and were converted. Boniface used the wood to build a chapel to St. Peter. That is the stuff of Christian Europe. ... A miracle here and a victorious battle there; and the Germans were ready for baptism."[18] *A wicked and corrupt generation seeks after signs*, the Lord told those who demanded such from Him.[19] While a state religion may be made by such mysticism, the Lord God builds His kingdom by faith in the Son by grace given by the Spirit, with wisdom and trust in the written Word.

In 751, Pope Zacharias I gave approval to the crowning of Pippin the Short as king of the Franks. Pippin was the successor of Charles Martel, and while not king, he was powerful. With the pope's approval of his ascension to the throne, "Pippin subdued the Lombards and gave portions of central Italy to the pope as his own

---

[17] Morrish, chapter 4
[18] Shelley, 162
[19] Matthew 16:4

possession. This was the beginning of the so-called "States of the Church" which have their modern symbol in the Vatican State over which the pope presides. History calls this gift by Pippin the "Donation of Pippin." This was one of the most important events in medieval history, for it established in the medieval mind the principle that the pope had the power to give kingdoms. It also gave the pope a temporal sovereignty." [20]

"In 962 a restored Empire (now called the Holy Roman Empire) emerged under Otto I."[21] He made the papacy subservient to the Emperor. "By 988, Rome had established its dogmas here [England], with its various corruptions. Penances were imposed on sinners, but the culprit could buy exemptions at a market value: thus a year's fasting could be bought for thirty shillings paid to the church, and sinning became a mere trifle, especially to the rich."[22] The Pope's yearly income was greater than that of any German Emperor. This "was bound to have a catastrophic effect on the believer when he pictured against this background the poor tent-maker Paul, or the still poorer fisherman Peter, coming with dusty sandals to Rome and bringing nothing with them but a deep and noble desire to preach Christ and to die for Christ."[23]

Shelley reported that the Romish religion grew as meetings were held to resolve problems and "bishops from the larger cities exercised authority in certain

---

[20] Duncan, 45
[21] Ibid, 51
[22] Morrish, chapter 4
[23] Adam, 14

matters over the pastors from smaller towns. As the church grew it adopted, quite naturally, the structure of the empire."[24] When a church grows naturally, it is being conformed to the pattern of the world. The local assembly must grow spiritually, feeding on the Word of God as the Spirit grants growth. Man cannot manage nor profit from this growth.

The eastern and western Churches had a history of disagreements, having squabbled over the date of Easter in the 2nd century and over questions about the nature of God in the following years. "Rome and Constantinople became natural rivals politically and religiously. Then the argument waxed bitter over a clause in the creed (filioque) and certain matters pertaining to worship in the mid part of the ninth century, the Pope and the Patriarch of Constantinople condemned each other."[25] Neither side would yield to the other as alleged supreme ruler of Christendom. In 1054 Leo IX of Rome and Michael Cerluarius of Constantinople excommunicated each other. "The more religion and politics became intertwined in the East, the less independent became the patriarch of the capital (Constantinople)."[26]

> Over the years Russia made the aesthetic glories of Orthodox Christianity her own. Gradually Moscow came to see herself as the leader of the Orthodox world. A theory developed that there had been one Rome, in Italy, that had fallen to the barbarians and to the Roman Catholic heresy.

---

[24] Shelley, 143
[25] Duncan, 57
[26] Shelley, 145

There had been a second Rome: Constantinople. And when that fell to the Turks, there was a third Rome: Moscow. The emperor took his title from the first Rome - Tzar is the same word as Caesar - just as he had taken his religion from the second.[27]

Each pope worked to increase the power of the papacy, based on the erroneous doctrine that the pope was the vicar[28] of Christ – ruling on earth as He ruled in heaven. In the 12th century, Gregory VII issued the following principles to enshrine the doctrine of the pope as Christ's vicar:

a. the pope can be judged by no-one;
b. the Roman church has never erred and never will err till the end of time;
c. the Roman church was founded by Christ alone;
d. the pope alone can depose and restore bishops;
e. he alone can make new laws, set up new bishoprics, and divide old ones;
f. he alone can translate bishops;
g. he alone can call general councils and authorize canon law;
h. he alone can revise his own judgements;
i. he alone can use the imperial insignia;

---

j. he can depose emperors;
k. he can absolve subjects from their allegiance;
l. all princes should kiss his feet;
m. his legates, even though in inferior orders, have precedence over all bishops; an appeal to the papal court inhibits judgement by all inferior courts; a duly ordained pope is undoubtedly made a saint by the merits of St Peter.[29]

When man fails to comprehend the biblical account of the nature of God and the nature of man, unless a man is indwelt by the Holy Spirit of the living God, he will deify man and imagine God to be much like man.[30] This accounts for the romish tradition of esteeming the pope as they do and imagining God to be so willing to share His glory with a creature.[31] At the same time as the elite within the romish church were elevated to near deity, the common people were considered as mere chattel – much as pagan religions do. Let all who claim Christ repent of this type of rebellion and submit to Him, as revealed in Scripture, that He and no man would be glorified in our lives, that we would treat all humans with the respect owed those who were made in God's image.[32]

Thomas Aquinas is iconic as the standard bearer for papist theology; his *Summa Theologica* was seen as "the

---

[29] Gregorii VII Regisrum , in E. Casper, quoted in R.W. Southern, *Western Society and the Church in the Middle Ages*, p. 102.
[30] Psalm 50:2
[31] Isaiah 42:8
[32] James 3:9

major textbook of Catholic theology. During this period the Catholic doctrine of the sacraments was standardized, and the argument for the truthfulness of Catholic teachings were developed in their more sophisticated forms."[33] Universities emerged and quickly devolved into forums for discussion of pertinent issues of the day, emphasizing man's role in the world. "Thus, politics, art, music, economics, and the other so-called humane disciplines began to take the center of the stage away from the more speculative theological concerns. The day of the humanist was arriving."[34]

Francis of Assisi was a product of this environment, focusing his life on the care of the poor. His view of God and of man were seriously flawed. His ideal "was that neither he nor his followers should possess anything. He was wedded to "Lady Poverty. ... He said that the happiest man was the man who had nothing."[35] People often attach humanity to their philosophies as a means to make the ideas seem more personal and effective at drawing people away from the Word of God.

As the cult of Rome matured and grew in power and influence in the world, the papacy "was almost unchallenged by any secular rulers. Pope Innocent III (1198 - 1216) wielded perhaps more power than any churchman ever has. ... he was able to call national kings to account for their moral delinquencies and sins. He virtually had all of Europe at his feet. He believed papal authority was the ultimate earthly and spiritual authority. ... Innocent also believed that the pope was

---

[33] Duncan, 62
[34] Ibid, 63
[35] Ibid, 63-64

the absolute ruler in the Church. The Church must represent the whole of Christianity, and it must be under one head. This idea naturally led to a papal dictatorship and, by implication, to the idea of his infallibility in doctrine." [36]

> During the pontificate of Innocent III. (1198-1216) the papacy rose to the zenith of its baleful authority. This greatest of all the popes, save Hildebrand, blasphemously appropriated to himself, as the pretended vicar of Christ, the words of the risen Jesus, "All power is given unto me in heaven and earth," and strove to realize them in Europe. To King John, of England, he said, "Jesus Christ wills that the kingdom should be priestly, and the priesthood kingly. Over all, he set me as his vicar upon earth, so that, as before Jesus 'every knee shall bow,' in like manner to his vicar all shall be obedient, and there shall be one flock and one shepherd. Pondering this truth, thou, as a secular prince, hast subjected thy realm to Him to whom all is spiritually subject. This claim Innocent made good throughout the greater part of Europe, here by skillful diplomacy, there by aid of the sword, elsewhere by the spiritual censures of the church. He humbled the pride of the kings of France and Spain, made and unmade emperors, and compelled England's most despotic monarch to bow the knee, surrender his

---

[36] Duncan, 65

realms "to God and the pope," and receive them back as a feudatory.[37]

Innocent III called the Fourth Lateran Council in 1215; the papal residence was at that time still in the Church of the Lateran. "All of Europe was awed by the great plans for the council, and great crowds poured into Rome during the spring and summer. The press of the throng was so great that at the first session the old Archbishop of Amalfi fell and was trodden to death. This was an occasion when many of the church men sought to impress others with their importance."[38] At this council, the doctrine of transubstantiation moved from mere practice to an article of faith. The self-important leaders also declared the Greek church to be subordinate to the Roman Church and they "further ordered bishops and archbishops to conduct an inquisition at least once a year to ferret out heresy in their domains. The particular objects toward which this measure was directed were the Albigensians and Waldensians. Innocent III actually launched a crusade against the Albigensians, seeking to destroy them by force of arms."[39]

Force of arms; the last resort of the false religion of the state-church, as the saints of the living God are not easily convinced to abandon the Lord that redeemed them, returning to the weak and beggarly elements of the world[40], no matter how nicely they may be wrapped up in the ribbons and bows of the sinful world.

---

[37] Henry Clay Vedder, *A Short History of the Baptists*, page 41
[38] Duncan, 66
[39] Ibid, 67
[40] Galatians 4:3

It is in Protestantism[41] that true catholicity is be found. The Romish church is not a catholic church. Separated from the churches of the east, which are the oldest in Christendom, and from the reformed churches, which are the purest, it is nothing but a sect, and that a degenerated one.[42]

Much of the best evidence demonstrating how false and hateful a religion has been built up by Rome is easily discovered in various Roman Catholic Churches around the globe. One example will suffice.

In 897 a trial took place at the Basilica San Giovanni Laterano in Rome, Italy. Pope Stephen VI tried Pope Formosus; or rather, the rotting carcass of what had been Pope Formosus, who had died a year earlier. "The trial was called the Cadaver Synod or *Synodus Horrenda* (since everything is more colorful in Latin). It ushered in one of the most corrupt eras in the history of the papacy, a time that's now referred to in all seriousness as the pornocracy[43]."[44]

Charlemagne's empire had collapsed and people were scrambling to enrich themselves in the chaos. Several men found themselves embattled against their fellow papists as they each sought to become pope. Pope John VIII was threatened by the advances of Bishop Formsus

---

[41] Editor: By "Protestantism" D'Aubigne means all who did not submit to Rome.
[42] J.H. Merle D'Aubigne, *History of the Reformation*, Volume Five, Book XIX, page 403
[43] A government by, or dominated by, prostitutes or corrupt persons.
[44] Atlas Obscura, https://www.atlasobscura.com/articles/morbid-monday-cadaver-synod

and found a legal avenue to excommunicate the bishop. "John's paranoia was justified. He was the first pope to be murdered by his own people. At first he was poisoned, but the poisoner lost patience waiting for the potion to take effect and bashed John's head in with a hammer. After John's death the papacy had such a high turnover rate, it's a wonder anyone wanted the job at all. Marinus I succeed John and re-instated Formosus as bishop. The following year Pope St. Adrian III succeeded Marinus, but barely lasted a year before being assassinated himself. Pope Stephen V followed shortly thereafter."[45] In 891, Formosus managed to get white smoke to confirm him as pope, holding that office for almost 5 years, until his death in 986.

> His successor, Boniface VI, was elected quickly to squelch riots, but he was an odd choice — he had been defrocked twice for "immoral conduct." He only ruled for 15 days before he died of either gout or poisoning (again). Next up was Pope Stephen VI. Less than a year into his papacy, he gave the order to dig up Formosus and force his corpse to stand trial for crimes Pope John VIII had excommunicated him for: seeking the papacy and ruling over more than one place a time as bishop.[46]

Formosus' corpse was dressed in papal robes and set in a chair to face his accusers. "A deacon was appointed to speak for him, but predictably didn't say much while Stephen screamed at the corpse. At one point in the trial

---

[45] Atlas Obscura, https://www.atlasobscura.com/articles/morbid-monday-cadaver-synod
[46] Ibid.

an earthquake shook the basilica, damaging part of it. But even in the face of this ominous sign, Formosus was found guilty on all counts, stripped of his vestments, and had the three fingers he used for blessing on his right hand chopped off. Stephen had him buried on an obscure plot of land, but then, thinking better of it, had him dug up one more time and tossed in the Tiber. At this point the people of Rome had just about enough of Stephen and his corpse trial. A mob threw him in prison where he was strangled in his cell. Later that year, San Giovanni Laterano was nearly destroyed by a fire as if to rid itself of the whole nasty business."[47]

"But the wicked are like the storm-tossed sea, for it cannot be still, and its waters churn up mire and muck. There is no peace for the wicked," says my God. (Isaiah 57:20-21) So it is in this life, and – more importantly – in the life to come, for all who do not know and follow the Lord Jesus.

One of the main-stays of the Roman Church is her system of monasteries. The shaving of the fore part of the head from ear to ear in the form of a crescent or (for Italians) a circle – allegedly in honor of the crown of thorns which was pressed upon the head of the Redeemer – was the sign Rome assigned to their monks. The monks were the keepers of the holy books and provided order in the small towns and rural areas where "big officials" cared not to live or visit. "The reader need scarcely be reminded how contrary monasticism is to Christianity. The plea raised for a monastic life, was that by its means greater holiness was attained; but it is

---

[47] Atlas Obscura, https://www.atlasobscura.com/articles/morbid-monday-cadaver-synod

manifest that, however earnest the desire to escape from the corruptions of the world, and indeed of the professing church, holiness is not to be obtained that way. All Christians have their old nature remaining in them, and this being carried by the monks into their cells, they may be as much engaged in serving the flesh there as in the world, and thus have as little practical holiness. Whereas the example of Christ was going about doing good. He also sent his disciples into the world (warning them to keep themselves free from its spirit and ways), and prayed that they might be kept from its evil. (John 17:15, 18.)"[48]

> Among the various monasteries that existed in the sixth century, we read of one near Mount Sinai in Arabia — a small place called the Prison. In this place the monks who had committed any great crime imprisoned themselves. They spent their time in prayer, with every possible self-denial and debasement. Not one single comfort did they allow themselves. In their prayers they did not consider they could ask for or expect entire forgiveness; but they besought that their punishment might not be to the utmost of their deserts. Voluntary punishments continued with many until their death.
>
> How strange that any who called themselves Christians should hope for forgiveness or an abatement of their punishment because of their austerities, instead of turning their eyes to the word of God — where they could have read that "if we confess our sins, he is faithful and just to

---

[48] Morrish, chapter 3

forgive us our sins, and to cleanse us from all unrighteousness." (1 John 1:9.)

Yet so little knew they of forgiveness of sins through the sacrifice of Christ, that the utmost they hoped for was less punishment than they merited for the sin they had committed. Of the true gospel they appear to have been entirely ignorant. And yet these were some of those deemed to be more holy than the mass of the Christians in those days: another proof of the darkness settling over Christendom.[49]

Spiritual darkness was spreading like a cancer across Europe as this ungodly state-church sought to increase her power and reach, while seeking to convert or kill all who confess Christ but would not submit to the papacy.

One of the most successful campaigns of Rome in her quest to increase her grip on the thrones of the nations was the much-misunderstood series of crusades to retake "the Holy Land." Still lost on so many Christians is the truth that the Kingdom of God is not of this world and has no holy places or holy days, but a holy people captured by the one Holy God. This was one of the truths Jesus revealed to the Samaritan woman in John 4.

"Sir," the woman replied, "I see that You are a prophet. Our fathers worshiped on this mountain, yet you Jews say that the place to worship is in Jerusalem." **Jesus told her, "Believe Me, woman, an hour is coming when you will worship the Father neither on this mountain nor in Jerusalem.** *You Samaritans worship*

---

[49] Morrish, chapter 3

*what you do not know. We worship what we do know, because salvation is from the Jews. But **an hour is coming, and is now here, when the true worshipers will worship the Father in spirit and truth.** Yes, the Father wants such people to worship Him. God is spirit, and those who worship Him must worship in spirit and truth."* (John 4:19-24)

But people are easily attached to what they can see and measure; so holy days and holy spaces have a hold on those who are not content to take God at His Word and fix their eyes on heavenly things rather than earthly things (Colossians 3:2). And in the Dark Ages, circumstances were ripe for the papacy to rally the faithful to push back the Muslim hoards and take back the Holy Land for God.

"Missions can proceed in two ways. One is the way of individual conversion with a period of instruction before baptism. ... The disadvantage of this method is that the Christian converts in a pagan culture become, by reason of their change in faith, uprooted from their own culture and compelled to move into an alien enclave. The other method is mass conversion, and it was this method that converted Europe. ... This meant that individuals were not uprooted from their culture, but it also meant that the converts brought with them into the church their superstitions and behavior."[50] The former method is what the Bible teaches; the latter is a product of man's wicked imagination, leaving people deceived about what life in Christ is truly about.

---

[50] Shelley, 167-168

As mentioned in the opening of this chapter, another force was active in Europe: the political system wrapped in religious clothes sought to conquer all who stood in its way. The rise and violent spread of Islam throughout Europe, Kennedy observed, was catastrophic in many ways, "yet it was not the spiritual movement of the church that suffered near extermination, but the proud ecclesiasticism which claimed dominion over the souls of men and offered to sacraments and idols the reverence that was due to God alone. Islam was God's judgment on pagan idolatry. It was a judgment upon Christian idolatry as well."[51]

Islam is a product of the Dark Ages; Muhammed was born in 570 and allegedly received a call from the angel Gabriel at age 40. Two years later, in 622, Islam emerged. When the Hadith was published, it revealed a system unreconcilable with the Christian faith[52]:

- Jesus is human
- Is a unique prophet, mentioned in 93 verses and 15 suras of the Qur'an
- Is called the Messiah, the Word of God, and the Spirit of God
- He is a prophet to the Jews
- Foretold the coming of Muhammad (John 14:26)

---

[51] Kennedy, 109

[52] The following is taken from a presentation titled "Islam & Christianity", by Don Closson.

The Quran teaches:

- (9:5) "Fight and slay the pagans wherever you find them, and seize them, beleager them, and lie in wait for them in every stratagem."
- (9:29) "Fight those who believe not in Allah nor the Last Day, nor hold that forbidden which hath been forbidden by Allah and His Prophet, nor acknowledge the religion of Truth, (even if they are) of the People of the Book, until they pay the jizyah with willing submission, and feel themselves subdued."
- (47:4-7) "When you meet unbelievers, smite their necks, then, when you have made wide slaughter among them, tie fast the bonds; then set them free, either by grace or ransom, till the war lays down its loads…And those who are slain in the way of God, He will not send their works astray. He will guide them, and dispose their minds aright, and He will admit them to Paradise, that He has made known to them."

Islam is a pagan system of government, based on dreams of a man shrouded in mystery, filled with hate for mankind, and spawning a cancer that has yet to be excised. Man cannot kill a cancer raised up by God as judgment and He will not end it until that judgment is complete.

The threatening cloud of Islam was accompanied with a further slide into superstition. "No period in church history, or perhaps in any history, or in any country, presents a darker picture than christian Europe at the close of the tenth century. The degradation of the papacy, the corrupt state of the church within, and the number and power of her enemies without, threatened her complete overthrow. Besides the unbelieving Mahometans in the East, and the pagan Northmen in the West, a new enemy the Hungarians — burst unexpectedly upon Christendom."[53] For several years, people gave up tending to earthly things – crops, houses, livestock, expecting the return of Christ by 999. When that failed to take place, they slowly resumed their former occupations.

Andrew Miller observed that the reason the papists focused attention on rescuing "the Holy Land" was not what it seemed. When Pope Urban II, in 1095, suggested this "holy war" and the Vatican agreed, it "was perfectly evident that by these long expeditions to Palestine, the blood of Europe must be drained, its strength exhausted, and its treasure wasted. There was no thought of seeking to convert the unbelieving to the faith of Christ — the true mission of Christianity — but of weakening the power of the temporal monarchs, that the pontiffs might reign over them."[54] When Urban announced this campaign publicly, he "offered absolution for all sins — the sins of murder, adultery, robbery, arson — and that without penance to all who would take up arms in this sacred cause. He promised eternal life to all who should suffer the glorious calamity of death in the Holy Land, or even on the way to it."[55] The crusades were primarily a tool to consolidate power in the papacy.

---

[53] Miller, 291
[54] Ibid, 318
[55] Ibid, 320-321

The first crusade was scheduled to begin on August 15th, 1096 and people across Europe began to make ready. "Property of all kinds was sold to raise money; but as all wanted to sell and none to buy, it naturally fell to an exceedingly low price, and was bought up chiefly by the clergy; so that nearly the whole property of the country passed into their hands."[56] This glorious war provided opportunity for peasants and outlaws and debtors to escape their dreary lives and participate in glory. The masses were growing anxious and impatient, waiting for August 15th.

Some 600,000 men, with countless support personnel, headed to "the Holy Land." They fought at Nicaea and Dorylium on their way, arriving at Antioch in October, 1097 – ten months after their departure. The siege lasted eight months; they arrived at Jerusalem in May of 1099 with about half the number of troops they started with. "As they drew nearer the object of their long and perilous journey, and recognized the sacred places, such as Tyre, Sidon, Caesarea, Lydda, Emmaus, and Bethlehem, their enthusiasm knew no bounds. But when an elevation was reached which gave them a full view of the holy city, a cry of, "Jerusalem! Jerusalem! God wills it! God wills it!" burst forth. All threw themselves on their knees, and kissed the sacred ground."[57]

For the first time since 637, Jerusalem was again in the hands of "Christians." But this was merely the opening salvo in the pope's strategy of becoming the ruler of Europe. In 1147 the Roman army was summoned for a second crusade, as the Muslims were again in

[56] Miller, 321
[57] Ibid, 325

Jerusalem. This time, two Kings, Louis VII of France and Conrad III of Germany, lent their support and joined the holy war – with over 900,000 troops. They retreated to Europe in 1149, with a small number. The pope's army had been decimated. "Their bones were whitening all the roads and deserts over which they had passed. A million had perished in less than two years. ... But the crafty abbot convinced the people that he had been quite right in all he said, and that the failure of the expedition was a fit chastisement for the sins of the Crusaders. Thus we see that the only effect of the second crusade was to drain Europe of a great portion of its wealth, and of the flower of its armies, without bettering the condition of Christians in the East."[58]

There were additional crusades in 1189, in which more than half a million "Christian warriors" died; and in the span of years from 1195-1270, a total of eight such campaigns, comprised of some five million "Christian warriors," many of whom perished. Miller observed that historians had many opinions about the crusades, yet agreeing that they had a profound impact Europe and Asia. Miller said, "They were the means, under the overruling providence of God, of changing the whole structure of society in this and other countries."[59] The vast distance between the poor and wealthy was shrunk, reducing many lords and barons to poverty, having to sell their estates. "**But the Papacy was the chief gainer by the Crusades. A vast accession of power, influence, and wealth, to the pope, the clergy, and the monastic institutions was the immediate result. And**

---

[58] Miller, 328
[59] Ibid, 330

this was the one grand object of the papal policy."[60] By promising to forgive the sins of those who fought in these wars, "the pope declared all temporal, civil, and social obligations dissolved, by taking the cross. Thus every tie was broken that binds society together, a new principle of obedience was substituted, and the pope became the liege lord of mankind."[61]

"The spirit of mammon had won such an ascendancy in the Curia that Pope Clement VII (1523-1534) ...was trying to make money from the sale of Cardinal's hats."[62] It was in this context one papist preacher, Geiler von Kaisersberg, observed, "It is no longer the Holy Ghost who appoints the rulers of the Church, but the devil, and for money, for favor and by bribery of the Cardinals."[63]

Such is the way of false teachers – promising what they cannot deliver to accumulate disciples, weakening those who do not submit by drawing their people away. This is the way of Satan, using religion to draw weak and natural men aside with promises of power and wealth.

"Religion was materialized. Pious interest was focused more on the "holy things" - relics - than on the sacraments, more on pilgrimages and flagellations than on attending the services of the Church, and most of all on indulgences. ... From the middle of the fifteenth century the Popes began to distribute indulgences for the dead." One "prelate" by the name of Peraudi had taught that "indulgence could be gained for the dead by

---

[60] Miller, 331
[61] Ibid, 331
[62] Adam, 13
[63] Ibid.

people living in mortal sin."[64] He was never censured by the papacy for this.

Another form of influencing illiterate people was adopted by Rome: architecture.[65] As with other forms of art, architecture is rich with meaning that is usually very subjective. The types and shadows revealed in the Mosaic Covenant clearly define what structure they were to build for worship, but there appears to be no biblical principles guiding us under the New Covenant as to the type of building we should use as we gather to worship the Lord. The early saints often met in houses, but is not prescribed as doctrine and there's no sense that houses were sacred for this purpose.

Church buildings have been described as reaching up to God, by use of high arches and bell towers and steeples, laid out in the form of a cross (cruciform floor plans); clearly an element of worship.

How did the cruciform, the cross-shaped floorplan, come into use?

> As the Western Roman Empire crumbled in the fifth century, illiteracy became the norm. The church was desperate to teach matters of doctrine and faith to a people who had neither access to Scriptures nor an ability to read them. The architectural layout of the worship edifice served as a tool. The church was built in the shape of a cross to teach that the foundation of the church was the cross of Christ. The church faced east

---

[64] Adam, 22-23

[65] ED: This section on architecture is taken from chapter 10 of my book, *Captive to the Word of God*.

because of an understanding that Christ would return to earth from the east (Matt 24:27).

At the head of the edifice were three windows to represent the Trinity as the head of the church. The center of the church (the dome) was elevated to signify that the heart of the cross was closest to heaven and the heart of God.[66]

It is clear from the description above that the church mentioned is the Roman Catholic Church. She did her best to keep her subjects illiterate and ignorant of the Bible. Simple graphics are less specific than the written word, leaving the people more susceptible to being deceived by an unbiblical false gospel. This is implicit in all use of religious art, including architecture.

Early in the fourth century Constantine the Great became Emperor, and in the course of his reign (from A.D. 312 to 337) he recognised Christianity, and made it the religion of the State. It then, of course, became requisite to provide places of public worship. Probably the Christians would have been, in many cases, reluctant to make use of heathen temples, and few temples, if any, were adapted to the assembling of a large congregation. But the large halls of the baths and the basilicas were free from associations of an objectionable character, and well fitted for large assemblages of worshippers. The basilica, at least in Italy, was followed, to the exclusion of all others, when new buildings were erected for

[66] Guide to the Stone Chapel, located at http://www.laniertheologicallibrary.net/ accessed 15 June 2013

the purpose of Christian worship; and during the fourth century, and several succeeding ones, the churches of the West were all of the basilica type.[67]

The basilica was a key product of the Ancient Roman and Greek pagan religious cultures, with notable examples in the early 4th century being the Thermae of Diocletian and the Basilica of Constantine. The inexpensive, low-tech construction and wide spread availability of existing buildings built as basilicas made for a natural fit for the newly legal Christian religion. "Essentially, the basilica consisted of a rectangular hall separated into three aisles by two rows of columns. The central part, or nave, was carried up above the roofs of the side aisles in order that celestory windows above the side aisle roofs might flood it with light. At the end of the nave was a large aspe, replacing the pagan Roman bema."[68] "In these Roman basilicas we find almost all the essential distinguishing marks of the Christian church building as a type – the nave and side aisles, the aspe and transept, the celestory lighting, the glorified altar, the separated choir."[69]

The Roman Catholic Church, being THE recognized church, built upon this basic form, adding grandiose decorations and architectural details over time; and in the 4th century, developed the cruciform plan that spread to saints all over Europe. With Rome's ecclesiastical model, their churches and associated buildings became

---

[67] T. Roger Smith and John Slater, *Classic and Early Christian Architecture,* ePub location 249.2
[68] Talbot Hamlin, *Architecture Through the Ages*, page 187
[69] Ibid, 190

town centers, the focus of most all activity in any given town; the better to control their subjects. Based on the basilica, "this type of church was the form and type that has continued in Eastern Christendom to the present day, and has undergone surprisingly little variation."[70]

When the Magisterial Reformers took over church buildings from the cult of Rome, modifications of architectural details (location of altar, pulpit, use of bell tower) were made; and the protestants adopted the *form* of a church building that has its roots in pagan Rome and the Roman Catholic Church because it was less expensive than building new, and – perhaps – because some still held some traditions learned from Rome.

While certain elements of these "traditional" church buildings may be properly used as a building used for Christian worship, it is unclear how we can be enthusiastic about spending money and constructing a building that echoes its historical roots in the city on seven hills and has no warrant in Scripture.

Considering the history of the architecture normally associated with Christian buildings, should the form developed by the Roman Catholic Church as an essential part of her ecclesiology and theology be considered good, something to be pursued, as an element of corporate worship? As in other aspects of our Christian lives, we must be willing to sacrifice the idols of our beloved traditions and presuppositions if they do not align with Scripture. We should *not* build doctrine and theology to support them if they are not clearly taught in the Word of God. At the 2016 Together for the

[70] Smith and Slater, ePub location 262.6

Gospel conference in Louisville, KY, Phillip Jensen (an Anglican from New Zealand) told Mark Dever (a Baptist), that the Baptist talk about the "sanctuary" rubbed him wrong. His sanctuary, Jensen said, was in heaven with Christ! The building was merely a rain shelter.

This is the right perspective, avoiding sacred spaces and buildings and rooms and avoiding talking about them as though they are sacred. There is One who is sacred. Those He has purchased are sacred. Our worship of Him is sacred. The circumstances of our meetings are not.

As for those who lead the world astray, it has been pointed out that false teachers are not the ones to blame, as Scripture tells us, *For the time will come when they will not tolerate sound doctrine, but according to their own desires, will multiply teachers for themselves because they have an itch to hear something new. They will turn away from hearing the truth and will turn aside to myths.* (2 Tim. 4:3-4) False teachers and cruel political masters are God's judgment on people who will not have Christ Jesus rule over them (see the parable of the 10 minas in Luke 19:11-27).

On that great and terrible day, when the Son of Man returns to judge the nations, separating the sheep and the goats, no one will be able to blame another for his rebellion against God. *For God's wrath is revealed from heaven against all godlessness and unrighteousness of people who by their unrighteousness suppress the truth, since **what can be known about God is evident among them, because God has shown it to them.** For His invisible attributes, that is, His eternal power and divine nature, **have been clearly seen since the creation of the***

world, being understood through what He has made. As a result, people are without excuse. (Romans 1:18-20)

Ever since the Fall, we have this natural tendency to blame someone else for our sin. But nothing is hidden from God's sight and there will be no refuge from the wrath of the Lamb on that day of great wrath (Revelation 6:15 – 17). Let us not trust in man, no matter his station or position. The Word of God is our rule for life and godliness (2 Peter 1:3), may the Lord keep us from drifting into idolatry and the religion of men.

The one who says he is in the light but hates his brother is in the darkness until now. The one who loves his brother remains in the light, and there is no cause for stumbling in him. But the one who hates his brother is in the darkness, walks in the darkness, and doesn't know where he's going, because the darkness has blinded his eyes. (1 John 2:9-11)

5. Theology amongst the Remnants

For you were once darkness, but now you are light in the Lord. Walk as children of light. (Ephesians 5:8)

While a few monks who desired the milk of the Word were tolerated within the Roman Church, "men like Adnold of Brescia, Peter de Bruys, and Henry of Lausanne were not so fortunate. These were men who opposed the wealth and temporal power of the Church. They gathered devoted followers, but the powerful ecclesiastical machine ran over them. Arnold was hanged, and Peter was burned."[1] Arnold's "great idea was, the complete separation of Church and State. The old papal edifice — the hierarchy, which had been rising into such vast proportions ever since the days of Constantine, and which, under Gregory VII, aspired to govern the whole world, and to bind all the nations of the earth as so many fiefs of St. Peter — he boldly maintained should be utterly demolished and swept from the face of the earth."[2]

Several groups of faithful believers have been preserved in written history, including the Bogomils and the Albigenses. Henry Clay Vedder made note that most (he says all) of the information on the Bogomils was "gained from their bitter enemies and persecutors. All such testimony is to be received with suspicion, and should be scrupulously weighed and sifted before we

---

[1] Duncan, 56
[2] Miller, 343

accept it. Where these prejudiced opponents did not knowingly misstate the beliefs of "heretics," they often quite misunderstood them, viewing these beliefs as they did through the distorting lenses of Roman or Greek Catholicism. ... We get our chief information about Bogomil doctrine from the writings of one Euthymius, a Byzantine monk who died in 1118, who wrote a learned refutation of these and other "heresies" of his time. His account is generally accepted by historians as substantially correct—a most uncritical conclusion."[3]

These saints were ridiculed by their opponents; the following is one example:

> The heretics in appearance are lamb-like, gentle, modest and quiet, and their pallor is to show their hypocritical fastings. They do not talk idly, nor laugh loudly, nor do they manifest any curiosity. They keep themselves away from immodest sights, and outwardly they do everything so as not to be distinguished from the Orthodox Christians, but inwardly they are ravening wolves. The people, on seeing their great humility think that they are orthodox, and able to show them the path of salvation; they approach and ask them how to save their souls. Like a wolf that wants to seize a lamb, they pretend at first to sigh; they speak with humility, preach, and act as if they were themselves in heaven. Whenever they meet any ignorant and uneducated man, they preach to him the tares of their teachings, blaspheming the traditions of the Holy Church. ... The wretched ones think that they know the

---

[3] Vedder, *A Short History of the Baptists*, 32

depth of the Scriptures and, [are] willing to comment on them.[4]

Christian reader: are you marked by these things? Are you "lamb-like, gentle, modest and quiet," do you refrain from "idle talk" and "immodest sights?" Such are the marks of those indwelt by the Holy Spirit; such are those who do not submit to the allure of a false gospel and the applause of men.

Vedder provides another perspective on this group, revealing that those called Bogomils *did* know the Scriptures and were willing to comment on them:

The most prominent man among the Bogomils toward the close of the eleventh century was a venerable physician named Basil. He is sometimes described as their "bishop"; he was really one of the "elders" or perfecti, and his preeminence was due to his learning and character, not to his official rank. The emperor Alexander Coitnenus I., was a bitter persecutor. He did not hesitate to lay a trap for Basil by inviting him to the imperial table and cabinet, and by pretending a deep interest in the Bogomil's views drew from his victim a full exposition of them. A scribe hidden behind tapestries took it all down, and then the perfidious emperor arrested his venerable guest and put him in prison. Basil was condemned and burned at the stake, to the last steadfast in his faith and meeting his cruel death with unfaltering trust in Christ. No charge was or could be brought against him, but his

---

[4] Cosmas, Sermon against Bogomilism, pages 108, 112

"heresy." To the elevation of his character and his life of good works even the daughter of the emperor, who recorded her father's shame, bore unwilling witness. We learn from her also that many families of the highest rank had embraced the Bogomil doctrines. At the height of their prosperity the credentes are said to have numbered two millions, and the perfecti perhaps four thousand. Through the early medieval times, therefore, down to the eleventh century, we find evangelical Christianity suppressed with virtual completeness throughout Europe. Even those forms of Christianity that may, in comparison with Rome, be called evangelical are far from bearing a close resemblance to the doctrine and practice of the apostles. No other conclusion can be drawn from a careful and impartial survey of all the evidence.[5]

In the early 13th century another group sharing similar concerns as the Waldensians sprang up in south-central France. The Albigensians, also known as the Cathari, "were influenced early by the eastern dualistic heretics, the Paulicians, and the Bogomiles. ... their doctrines were more remote from the central stream of Christian teaching than those of the Waldensians."[6] The large number of defectors from Rome in southern France prompted "Dominic of Spain to organize a group of followers into a movement expressively designed to win the common people back to the fold of Rome. ... they took vows of poverty, celibacy, and obedience as other

---

[5] Vedder, *A Short History of the Baptists*, 33
[6] Duncan, 65

monastics, but they did not separate themselves from the common activities of everyday life."[7]

In the early 13th century, the papist cult had defeated the Albigenses and settled into a routine of ruling. Earl Remond, one of the Albigenses' leaders, was forced to sign a treaty which contained these, among other terms:

> 1. Everyone identified as an Albigenses had to pay a mark of silver; any who failed to pay and cling to their faith were be put to death, their goods forfeited, their wills nullified – leaving nothing for their families.
>
> 2. Their houses were to be demolished, leaving them homeless.[8]

Kennedy reviews the lives of several men who were identified with the Paulicians, and notes that they refuted the idea that any of these men were responsible for their identity - such was the work of God through means He had appointed. This aligns with Paul's admonition in 1 Corinthians 3, wherein he says God gives the increase and neither the one who plants nor the one who waters is anything, but only God who gives the growth. This attitude is in dire need in our day, as Christians are too eager to build their work around a man. It's easy to point to Joel Osteen but my fellow Baptists are just as guilty, with their love for "senior pastors" and so-called "mega-churches" with the names of wealthy congregants plastered on pews and sidewalks and buildings. Such boasting in men is not healthy.

---

[7] Duncan, 65
[8] Perrin, 223

One of these Paulician men, Constantine Silvanus, lived in the 7th century and had been brought to faith in Christ by reading the Scriptures. "Testifying of the new life he had received, he soon found fellowship with groups of people of a like experience who rejected the idolatry and superstition of the organized Church, and met together in accordance with what he himself had learned from his study of the Scriptures. ... In 684 the Byzantine Emperor, alarmed by the success of Silvanus and the increase of the Paulicians, issued a decree against them. ... and Silvanus was stoned to death. ... The Fires of persecution but served to strengthen the faith, courage, and devotion of the believers. Preachers and teachers were raised up to take the place of those who had given their lives for their Lord, and the congregations increased." [9]

"The middle of the ninth century saw the notorious persecution under the Empress Theodora. Within a space of five years it is said that a hundred thousand persons met their death in the wave of indescribable terror."[10] Kennedy notes that some of the Paulicians succumbed to the fleshly notion of taking up weapons against their persecutors, and he soberly observed, "Where God's people can be persuaded to press their claims to their own rights in this unjust and sinful world as a matter of prime importance, soon fleshly means will be employed, and the churches will be rendered spiritually impotent."[11]

---

[9] Kennedy, 111-112
[10] Ibid, 114
[11] Ibid.

In 1229, a "council called to address a growing neo-gnostic movement in southern France known as the Albigensians, a group of Christians in southern France in the 12th and 13th centuries who were ruled heretics by the Catholic Church. The council concluded that nobody in the area should possess copies of the Bible, especially vernacular (ED: common language) translations. All such copies were to be burned and the homes of those in possession of them were also to be burned."[12] It is commonplace in warfare to describe your opponents in unfavorable, often sub-human terms; makes it easier to kill them when you stop thinking of them as fellow human beings made in the image of God. Hence the Church of Rome termed all who did not bow to her as heretics of one stripe or another, to dull the senses of her subjects.

This prohibition of owning the Bible was initially aimed at the Albigensians but was in effect throughout the Roman Catholic's empire, including England. This lack of Scripture in a common tongue aggravated the literacy problem by insuring spiritual ignorance as well.[13]

England came under the rule of the papacy as the result of a dispute in the early 13th century between King John and Canterbury regarding selection of an archbishop. Pope Innocent III declared King John's selection null and void and installed his own man, Cardinal Langton, as archbishop. King John saw this as a threat to the monarchy and he ordered all the pope's men out of the

---

[12] https://historyofchristiantheology.com/glossary/council-of-toulouse/
[13] Steve Burchett, *Wycliffe: A Bible Man in England When There Was No English Bible*, page 6

kingdom. Innocent responded with an interdict, closing church buildings and ceasing all religious activities. After two years, the pope excommunicated John and offered the crown of England to Philip Augustus, King of France. John had lost the support of the people and barons; he surrendered England and Ireland to Innocent and his successors – stipulating that any of John's successors who fail to abide would forfeit all right to rule. This was memorialized on 15 May, 1213. This aroused the barons of England to take up arms in defense of ancient English liberties. On June 15th, 1215, they forced John to sign the Magna Carta at Runnymede, breaking his agreement with Rome.[14]

But Rome still had a presence all over Europe. Localities had Papist friars stationed within them; these men took vows of poverty but they extorted money from the townsfolk, begged for food, "and taught mystical stories and entertaining fables from village to village. Bible stories and legends were not distinguished, and even blended together. More darkness in 14th century England is uncovered when considering the entanglement of the church and state."[15] Things were gloomy for England as the next century opened. "In 1400, it became law in England that heretics were to be burned – and the emissaries of Rome got to work. William Santree, a follower of Wycliffe, was the first victim; followed by John Badby, who was a common man who denied transubstantiation. The English "clergy drew up the well-known Constitutions of Arundel,

14 David J. Deane, *John Wicliffe, the Morning Star of the Reformation*, pages 10-12
15 Burchett, 7

which forbade the reading of the Bible and the books of Wycliffe, asserting the pope to be "not of pure man, but of true God, here on the earth." Persecution now raged in England; a prison in the archiepiscopal palace at Lambeth, which received the name of the Lollards' tower, was crowded with the followers of Wycliffe."[16]

The begging friars of Rome were founded as the Franciscans and Dominicans. "The Dominicans were divided into two companies; the one went forward to convert heretics, the other, by the terrible power of the inquisition, to slay them."[17] "The Franciscans by pious frauds endeavoured to monopolise the wealth of the country. "Every year," they said, "St. Francis descends from heaven to purgatory and delivers the souls of all those who were buried in the dress of his order." ... These friars used to kidnap children and shut them up in monasteries."[18]

The inquisition was a means to hold people in a state of terror, not knowing when or where a loved one might be arrested for inquiries, maybe to disappear never to be seen again. "The inquisitor played on the conscience, on the affections, on the hopes and fears of his victim, with cynical disregard of every moral law and inflicting the most exquisite mental tortures, in the hope of securing a confession."[19]

> Finally, if all other means failed, the inquisitors had another device for encouraging (such was their grim word) the accused to confess. That was

---

[16] Miller, 484

[17] Deane, 36

[18] Ibid, 37

[19] Vedder, *A Short History of the Baptists*, 44

physical torture—the rack, the thumbscrew, the boot, cautery in various forms, every infernal machine that could be devised to produce the most excruciating agony without unduly maiming or killing. ... Only in one way could he be certain of saving his life, and that was by a full confession at once, accompanied by a recantation of his errors and abject submission to the church. Then his life would be spared, but more likely than not it would be spent in some dungeon; only in rare cases was one who once fell into the clutches of the Inquisition suffered to return to his home and estate; and in those rare cases he was subject to life-long espionage and harassment.

When the process was completed and the accused was found guilty of heresy—which was the normal ending of a case—the inquisitors handed the heretic over to the civil power for punishment, with a hypocritical recommendation to mercy. But woe to the secular authority that heeded the recommendation! If a magistrate failed for twelve months to put to death a condemned heretic, the refusal itself constituted heresy, and he became subject to the kind offices of the Inquisition. Even if he were excommunicated, the magistrate must do his duty. The church, with characteristic evasion of the truth, claims to this day that it has never put a heretic to death. The claim is technically correct, if we except those who died in its dungeons and torture-chambers; but the church coerced the civil power into becoming its executioner, and therefore its moral responsibility is the same. When the heretic was dead, the vengeance of the church was not sated. All his lands and goods were confiscated, his blood was attainted, his family were beggared, if they did not share his fate, and his name was blotted out of existence— life, property, titles, all disappeared."[20]

In contrast to the duplicity and evil that characterized the Roman religion,

> The common people of the Middle Ages were not much given to subtlety of reasoning, but they judged the two trees by their fruits. They looked at the church and beheld rapacity, oppression, wickedness, from highest to lowest in the hierarchy; they looked at these heretical teachers and saw them to be such as Jesus was when upon earth— poor, humble, meek, pure, counting not life itself dear unto them if they might by any means win some. And by thousands and tens of thousands, men turned their backs upon such a church and accepted the teachings of such heretics.

> And these teachings were nothing less than revolutionary. They denied that tradition has any authority, they flung aside as rubbish all the writings of the Fathers, all the decrees of councils, all the bulls of popes, and taught that only the Scriptures, and especially the Scriptures of the New Testament, are authoritative in questions of religion, whether of faith or of

---

[20] Vedder, *A Short History of the Baptists*, 45

practice. They denied the efficacy of the sacraments, maintaining that that which is born of the flesh is flesh, and that which is born of the Spirit is spirit; and therefore denying that an inward spiritual change can by any possibility be produced by an outward physical act. They were Lutherans before Luther, in teaching justification by faith and not by works; and more radical and consistent than Luther in accepting the legitimate consequences of their doctrine; for they rejected the baptism of infants as alike unwarranted by Scripture, and absurd in itself, if sacramental grace be denied. These are the distinctive teachings of Baptists today, and the men who held these truths from the twelfth century onward, under what various nicknames it pleased their persecutors to give them, were our spiritual ancestry, our brethren in the faith.[21]

Among these so-called heretics, "in the Middle Ages the idea arose that every Christian needed to know three things: the Apostles' Creed as the summary of Christian belief, the Lord's Prayer as the model for Christian prayer, and the Ten Commandments as the guide for Christian behavior. These three items became the staple for Christian education during the period, and most of the catechetical material of the time used them as its basis."[22]

Another light was flickering in England, as a man known to us as John Wycliffe was born, around 1330. He was raised to believe in the papist religion and went

---

[21] Vedder, *A Short History of the Baptists*, 42
[22] Howard Hageman, *God and the Good*, page 36

to Oxford University when he was sixteen or so, to study for the Roman Catholic priesthood. Wycliffe was fluent in Latin and studied logic and philosophy; there was no requirement to study the Bible in preparation for the priesthood.[23] He fell in with a professor, Thomas Bradwardine, who "was one of the greatest mathematicians and astronomers of his day; but besides this he was deeply versed in the truths of Scripture, and as a theologian he became more renowned than he had been as a philosopher. He unfolded to his students the way of life, and warned them against substituting a worship of mere external forms and ceremonies in place of the true worship of the heart."[24] Other Christians and the Bubonic Plague (which killed two-thirds of the people in Wycliffe's hometown) were used by Almighty God to awaken young Wycliffe to eternal things which can only be learned aright from the Scriptures.[25]

When Wycliffe became a doctor of theology at Oxford, he had the "freedom to lecture on theology. Unlike so many who had gone before him who focused on Aquinas and Duns Scotus and the Sentences of Peter Lombard, Wycliffe taught the Bible."[26] Wycliffe became known as the "Gospel Doctor."[27] This belief that God has spoken and given us a written record is foundational to the Christian faith and opposed by any religion that rests on extra-biblical spiritual revelation.

Wycliffe gained favor in the eyes of King Edward III, as the King was fond of Wycliffe's opposition of

[23] Deane, *20*
[24] Ibid, 19
[25] Burchett, 13
[26] Ibid, 18
[27] Deane, 21

England sending money to the Pope, who had demanded Edward resume the annual tribute promised under King John. Wycliffe was appointed as King Edward's representative to the Pope, to meet in Bruges, France, in 1374. "Wycliffe's two years of service in Bruges on behalf of the King revealed to him more than ever the abuses of the Roman Catholic Church. He was further motivated to speak the truth and expose such depravity."[28] When religion seeks to grow by use of the sword and/or union with the state, it ceases to be Christian and will spiral into an ongoing pattern of persecution of those who see the Bible as adequate and complete.

Wycliffe published a tract, "Objections to Friars" around 1382, in which he laid open some 50 heresies taught by these papists. "The friars claimed, in the name of the Pope, to grant men pardon for their sins. The fallacy of this claim he exposed, but, at the same time, he pointed them to Him who alone could grant pardon for sin. "There cometh," said he, "no pardon but of God. There is no greater heresy than for a man to believe that he is absolved from his sins if he give money, or if a priest lay his hand upon his head and say that he absolveth thee; for thou must be sorrowful in thy heart and make amends to God, else God absolveth thee not.""[29]

Wycliffe was not always a dour-faced grumbler against the Roman Church, he "knew how to make his views known through unconventional and even humorous ways. For example, he said the letters in the title for the office of CARDINAL stood for this: "Captain of the

---

[28] Burchett, 27
[29] Deane, 42

Apostates of the Real of the Devil, Impudent and Nefarious All of Lucifer.""" [30]

In opposing the pope and his minions, Wycliffe was exposed to great hazards. "Their power was immense. For nearly two centuries the inquisition had been performing its work of torture and destruction on the Continent."[31] "But while the danger was great, the good that resulted from this controversy was also great. The mendicants pleaded the sanction of the Saviour for their begging. "Christ and His apostles," said they, "were mendicants and lived on alms." Men turned to the New Testament to see if it were so, and thus became more deeply acquainted with the Word of God. Wicliffe[32], especially, was led to a yet closer study of the Bible. The truths of Scripture were revealed to him more and more plainly, and he was led to see how widely the Church of Rome had departed from the Gospel of Christ."[33]

In 1377, Wycliffe was ordered by the Roman Bishop of London to appear at Our Lady's Chapel in St. Paul's to answer for his work. This court was as "just" as the trial of Jesus. At the end of it, "he was dismissed with an injunction against preaching his doctrines. But this decision of the priests was not ratified by the people of England. Public opinion declared in favour of the reformer. 'If he is guilty,' said they, 'why is he not punished? If he is innocent, why is he ordered to be silent. If he is the weakest in power he is the strongest in truth!" The issues of this affair were favourable to the Reformation. The cause of Wicliffe began to be more widely discussed and better understood by the nation.

---

[30] Burchett, 35

[31] Deane, 42

[32] ED: the proper spelling of Wycliffe's name is uncertain.

[33] Deane, 43

The designs of his enemies had been thwarted, but their hostility increased."[34]

A year later, Wycliffe was summoned by an agent of the pope to appear in court to again answer for his work. The setting was the Archbishop's Chapel at Lambeth. After many days, a lengthy list of charges was brought against the Gospel Doctor; he submitted the following written response:

> In the first place, I protest publicly, as I have often done, that I resolve with my whole heart, and by the grace of God, to be a sincere Christian; and, while life shall last, to profess and to defend the law of Christ as far as I have power. If through ignorance, or from any other cause, I shall fail in this determination, I ask forgiveness of God, and, retracting the errors, submit with humility to the correction of the Church. And since the notions of children, and of weak persons, concerning what I have taught, are conveyed by others, who are more than children, beyond the seas, even to the Court of Rome, I am willing to commit my opinions to writing. These also I am ready to defend even unto death. In my conclusions I have followed the sacred Scriptures and the holy doctors, both in their meaning and in their modes of expression: this I am willing to show; but should it be proved that such conclusions are opposed to the faith, I am prepared very willingly to retract them.[35]

---

[34] Deane, 57-58
[35] Ibid, 65-66

In light of all the cruel charges thrown at him by Rome, Wycliffe remained true to the calling of God paid upon his life. "Wicliffe was a true pastor. He preached the Gospel to the poor, and ministered by the bedside of the sick and dying, whether freeman or slave."[36] This is pastoral work of an elder – caring for the people of God. Merely standing before them to teach the Word is not what it takes to be pastoral.

When he started translating the Bible, only the Psalms and a few Old Testament books had been fully translated into English. The goal of translating these was to provide aid to the clergy, not to make them available to the common people.[37] Using the Latin Vulgate as his source, Wycliffe was, "slavishly literal – even to the point of retaining the Latin word order when it made no sense in English!" Therefore, Wycliffe's assistant, John Purvey, revised it twice (first in 1388, then in 1395) into more readable English." This desire to put the Word of God into the hands of common folk, as the Brits were in that day, guided every step Wycliffe took. Wycliffe was convinced the Bible was essential, not because of his work but because, "Spiritual profit is infinitely better than temporal, and spiritual profit cannot be acquired apart from the teaching of the Holy Scripture."[38]

This motive, to put the Word of God into the hands of the common folk, is evident in his work as Wycliffe endeavored to show the value of Bible knowledge by Christians; this being the means by which the Spirit gives wisdom.

---

[36] Deane, 73

[37] Ibid, 77

[38] Burchett, 51

In his treatise on the "Truth and Meaning of Scripture," he maintained the sufficiency of Christ's law for all purposes of doctrine, discipline, and daily conduct; and he argued "that a Christian man, well understanding it, may gather sufficient knowledge during his pilgrimage upon earth; that all truth is contained in Scripture; that we should admit of no conclusion not approved there; that there is no court beside the Court of Heaven; that though there were a hundred Popes, and all the friars in the world were turned into cardinals, yet should we learn more from the Gospel than we should from all that multitude; and that true sons will in no wise go about to infringe the will and testament of their Heavenly Father.[39]

In our day of print-on-demand and the easy, inexpensive availability of digital books, all made fairly easy with powerful word processors and desktop publishing, it is hard to grasp the task of printing and publishing before the printing press was invented. "It would be about a half a century before the printing press was available (1440), so every Wycliffe Bible had to be handwritten! Working full time, an entire Bible could take close to a year to finish."[40]

Historians estimated that 25 percent of the English population at the end of the 14th century viewed Wycliffe favorably. "How did this happen? John Wycliffe had disciples. These were chiefly Oxford graduates trained by Wycliffe himself, and sent by him all over the land to preach a plain and simple faith. Their

---

[39] Deane, 78
[40] Burchett, 47

commission was to preach the gospel; not to dispense pardons or celebrate Masses for the living or the dead. As time passed, even uneducated men were trained and became part of this traveling team of gospel preachers. ... Their aim was to communicate the truth plainly wherever they could ... with the goal that people would be converted to Christ." [41]

Early in 1381, Wycliffe published twelve propositions against the papist doctrine of transubstantiation. "The first of these theses was as follows: "The consecrated host which we see upon the altar[42] is neither Christ nor any part of Christ, but an efficacious sign of him. Wicliffe argued that the bread and wine were as truly bread and wine after as before their consecration."[43] A council of Roman officials was formed to, once again, try Wycliffe. An officer of the court read the condemnation passed against him by the council. "For a moment he remained silent, he then rose and said, "You ought first to have shown me that I am in error," and then he challenged his opponents to refute his published opinions. Receiving for reply that he must either submit to silence or imprisonment, he said, "Then I appeal to the King and the Parliament.""[44]

In November of 1382, Parliament was assembled; an appeal was made to repeal a law passed at the behest of Rome, which condemned Wycliffe's work. The King granted this request. The Parliament and papal Convocation met, this time at Oxford. Wycliffe was ordered to appear before the Convocation; it had been

---

[41] Burchett, 55-56
[42] ED: This is another sign of pagan religion – the altar. In the New Covenant, there is no altar other than Christ Himself (Heb. 13:10)
[43] Deane, 85
[44] Ibid, 86

forty years since he first entered Oxford as a student. Its "halls had witnessed the toils of his youth and the labours of his manhood; but now it appeared to be turning against him."[45]

Simply to be given a fair hearing in front of parliament was too much an honor to be given a "heretic" like Wycliffe. Such activity was sure to provoke the monster state-church on both sides of both sides of the English Channel – as when Rome rose up against the Albigenses a century earlier. "Wycliffe's enemies were incensed. They knew, as Wallace writes, that a Bible in the vernacular "indirectly began to break down the power structures of the political-religious machinery of the Roman Catholic Church. Lay folks did not need to rely on the priests to access God. And they could know his will and even challenge their spiritual leaders.""[46]

Oxford loomed large in Wycliffe's shadow. In 1408 the third synod held there banned unauthorized English translations of the Bible and decreed that possession of English translation's had to be approved by diocesan authorities. The Oxford council declared:

> It is dangerous, as St. Jerome declares, to translate the text of Holy Scriptures out of one idiom into another, since it is not easy in translations to preserve exactly the same meaning in all things. We therefore command and ordain that henceforth no one translate the text of Holy Scripture into English or any other language as a book, booklet, or tract, of this kind lately made in the time of the said John Wyclif or since, or that hereafter may be made, either in part or wholly, either publicly or privately, under

---

[45] Deane, 93
[46] Burchett, 48

pain of excommunication, until such translation shall have been approved and allowed by the Provincial Council. He who shall act otherwise let him be punished as an abettor of heresy and error.[47]

When the people of God have His Word in their language, the religion of the world is threatened. God's children will no longer be content to be merely the subjects of religious men. The living hope of Christ in them, the guidance of His Spirit through the Word gives strength to endure in the face of great hostility. They heard their Master when He said, "*Don't fear those who kill the body but are not able to kill the soul; rather, fear Him who is able to destroy both soul and body in hell.*" (Matthew 10:28) May we listen to our King with willing hearts and live as though we believe Him!

See how the enemies of the saints regarded them. The following opinion in regard to the antiquity of the Waldenses was rendered through one of the Austrian inquisitors in the Diocese of Passau, about the year 1260 (Preger, Beitrage zur Geschichte der Waldesier, 6-8). He says:

Among all the sects, there is no one more pernicious to the church than that of the Leonists (Waldenses), and for three reasons: In the first place, because it is the most ancient: for some say that it dates back to the time of Sylvester (A. D. 825); others to the time of the apostles. In the second place, because it is the most widespread. There is hardly a country where it does not exist. In the third place, because if other sects strike

---

[47] The Western Watchman, August 9, 1894, https://rodiagnusdei.wordpress.com/tag/council-of-tarragona/

with horror those who listen to them, the Leonists, on the contrary, possess a great outward appearance of piety. As a matter of fact they lead irreproachable lives before men and as regards their faith and the articles of their creed, they are orthodox. Their one fault is, that they blaspheme against the Church and the clergy, —points to which laymen In general are known to be too easily led away (Gretscher, Contra Valdenses, IV.).[48]

As the Reformation dawned, many who had been used of God would be forgotten by men, replaced by other men. But the faithful One keeps all those given to Him by the Father. We know nothing about what most of the apostles did and taught, but we know that each of them was foundational to the New Covenant community (Ephesians 2:20). This ought to encourage us to serve God for His glory without regard to making a name for ourselves.

Then Jesus spoke to them again: "I am the light of the world. Anyone who follows Me will never walk in the darkness but will have the light of life." (John 8:12)

---

[48] John T. Christian, *A History of the Baptists, Volume I*, page 45

6. Dawn of the Reformation

The people who live in darkness have seen a great light, and for those living in the shadowland of death, light has dawned. (Matthew 4:16)

The Reformation is clouded with mystery as is most of history – records are incomplete and biased. Many say the Reformation began when Martin Luther nailed his 95 theses against indulgences on the door of the Wittenberg church building. In truth, this was a narrow protest that hit at the heart of the papist cult, which was using indulgences to convince ignorant, superstitious people to pay money to shorten time in purgatory for loved ones – so the pope could build St. Peter's cathedral. The movement which produced the Reformation was in YHWH's slow cooker for many years prior to this, as His Spirit moved His people to cling to His Word and proclaim it far and wide in the face of fierce rebellion from the prince of the power of the air.

> On the eve of the Reformation everything was on the decline—faith, life, light. It was so of the Waldenses. Persecution had wasted their numbers and had broken their spirit and the few scattered leaders were dazed by the rising glories of the Reformation. The larger portion had gone with the Anabaptist movement. Sick and tired of heart in 1530 the remnant of the Waldenses opened negotiations with the Reformers, but a

> union was not effected till 1532. Since then, the
> Waldenses have been Pedobaptists.[1]

Several people bridged the Dark Ages to the
Reformation. One of these was John[2] Hus of Husinec,
Bohemia; he took his last name from his native home,
in accordance with the custom of the time – late 14th
century. "The family name of Hus is not known. His
parents were peasants of scanty means. They
endeavoured to give John, who was his mother's
favourite son, a good education. He had brothers and
sisters. Nothing is known of them, except that about the
sons of a brother he manifested a touching concern even
during the last days of his life."[3]

Hus' family was not wealthy, but his parents resolved to
educate John well, after the monks training him noted
his intelligence. He was sent to a school in a nearby
town and John decided he would attend university; he
studied theology at the University of Prague where the
conflict was between the colloquial religion of Bohemia
and the Roman Catholic religion.

At this time, Rome had two popes, "each claiming to be
the rightful representative of Christ on earth, were
denouncing each other in no measured terms."[4] This
confusion among the religious elite prompted Hus and
other men "to make a clear understanding of the
Scriptures the great purpose of their lives. In the
writings of various devout men they saw signs of hope.
Particularly, in the works of Wyclif, which at this time

---

[1] Christian, 53
[2] Native spelling of his first name is "Jan."
[3] W. N. Schwarze, *John Hus - The Martyr of Bohemia*, page 28
[4] Ibid, 32

were brought to the attention of the university, did they recognize a man whose daring views and Scriptural method of reform were to confirm powerfully their own bent of mind."[5]

Hus persevered and earned a Master's degree; two years later, he was called to serve at the University of Prague as a professor. "Hus searched for truth, and the truth as he found it in the Bible was the foundation on which he built. So long as he saw no difference between the teachings of the Scriptures and the doctrines of the Church, he did not antagonize the latter. Whenever any disagreement was plain, he followed the Scriptures."[6] Hus' skill as a preacher was recognized and in 1401, he was chosen to serve as Father Confessor to Queen Sophia, wife of King Venceslas of Bohemia. This provided him with favor in high places where he gained powerful friends.

Hus obtained an appointment to be the preacher at the Bethlehem Chapel in Prague, large enough to seat up to 3,000 people. "The pulpit of the Bethlehem Chapel became for him a throne of power. For twelve years he wielded from it an influence exceeding that of archbishop or king. The former preachers had been renowned for their eloquence. The fame of the Chapel became even greater when Hus began to preach there. Crowds thronged to hear him. They represented every class of society."[7] This was before the printing press,

---

[5] Schwarze, 32
[6] Ibid, 33-34
[7] Ibid, 35

making this pulpit the most powerful platform in the nation at that time.

During his second year at Bethlehem Chapel, Hus was asked by the university to examine Wycliffe's writings, as they were widespread in Prague and condemned as heresy in London. Hus was not familiar with Wycliffe and the fact his work was condemned piqued Hus' interest; and he read. "As, at the same time, conditions in Church and state drove him to acquire further knowledge of the truth and as he became convinced of the Biblical character of many of the views of Wyclif, he read with increasing sympathy and enthusiasm. He was fast losing his early horror of what was called heresy in Wyclif."[8]

This theological conflict Hus found himself in prompted him to write, as he desired his countrymen to be free of the corrupt doctrine of Rome. One of his first publications was a translation of Wycliffe's *Trialogue*, considered to be the Englishman's doctrinal system. "One of the largest and most important of Hus's Latin works is his *Super IV Sententiarum,* a commentary on the sentences of Peter Lombard. This then world-famed book - written in the eleventh century - was for many generations the recognized textbook of theology. It consisted of a vast collection of the opinions of the fathers of the Church on all matters of faith. Judged by his extensive commentary on this work, Hus was a true scholar, a man of great learning."[9]

Hus' time at Bethlehem Chapel ended because he found less and less ground for peace with Rome. The books of

---

[8] Schwarze, 41-42
[9] Ibid, 43

heretics, including Wycliffe, were burned in Prague by order of the pope. "It was meant to be the end of trouble. By God's providence it proved the beginning of sorrows. A large proportion of the citizens of Prague were enraged. A cry of indignation rose throughout Bohemia. … It is a great tribute to the power and influence of Hus that in such a condition of the community, apart from some instances of imprudence, order was generally maintained. … His words thrilled the hearts of his hearers as he exclaimed, "Fire does not consume truth. It is always a mark of a little mind to vent anger on inanimate and uninjurious objects.""[10]

Pope John XXIII of the early 15th century was a self-appointed pope, termed "anti-pope" by the modern Roman Catholic religion. He demanded Hus travel the 1,200 miles to Rome and answer the charge of heresy. Hus saw nothing to be gained by appearing before this rogue pope, who hated him for speaking against the Roman religion. The cost of the trip and absence from his congregation swayed him to remain home, sending a few men in his stead. This accomplished nothing. "When the term fixed for his personal appearance had expired, the decree of excommunication was issued against him. This decree was published in nearly all the parish churches of Prague, in March, 1411."[11]

John Wycliffe sent the Bohemian a letter, to encourage him in his battle for the Bible. "Hus took it into the pulpit and read it to his congregation. Coming from so distant a country as England, it was received with great enthusiasm by the large number of people assembled."[12]

---

[10] Schwarze, 57
[11] Ibid, 60
[12] Ibid

Hus wrote back, saying, "Know, dearest brother, that our people will hear nothing but Holy Scripture, particularly the evangels and epistles, and whenever in a city or town, cottage or castle, a preacher of holy truth appears, the people flock together, despising the evilly-disposed clergy."[13] All this was maddening to the archbishop, who "proclaimed an interdict over the city of Prague. ... The interdict was one of the most powerful and dreaded weapons of the Romish Church. It was a kind of public excommunication of the entire city and its surroundings."[14]

An interdict closed off all Romish buildings and practices to everyone in the affected area, meaning no burials in church yards, no public services, no church bells. "A general appearance of mourning and fasting had to be assumed by the populace. ... This terrible weapon brought matters to a crisis. The king now authoritatively interfered. He appointed a commission to which the whole matter was referred. Both parties pledged themselves to submit to its decision."[15] Although agreement was reached in principle, the document was lost in the mail and when the archbishop died, his successor continued to seek to bring Hus before his court; he introduced the sale of indulgences to Prague in hopes of provoking Hus.

Ultimately, Hus appeared before the court of Rome held in Prague on June 17, 1412. The question put forth asked if the bulls of the pope were in accordance with "the law of Christ, the glory of God, and the salvation of Christian people."[16] Hus "proved conclusively that

---

[13] Schwarze, 60
[14] Ibid, 61
[15] Ibid, 60-61
[16] Ibid, 69

the papal bull ran counter to the Holy Scriptures and was an outrage upon Christianity. ... He saw in the act of the pope abuse of sacred interests. His spirit glowed with the resolute purpose to unmask the false pretensions and evil principles of the crusade and the indulgences. Yet he spoke and acted quietly as well as firmly."[17] Nothing was settled but the fire had been stoked and Rome's ire was burning hot. Later that year, at the urging of a papal minion named Michael de Causis, a "papal bull was published excommunicating Hus in the severest form known to the papacy."[18] It was forbidden to all to provide any food or comfort to Hus and, at the end of 23 days he was to be excommunicated. Another papal bull was issued, commanding her subjects "to seize the person of Hus and deliver him up to the archbishop to be burned. The bull, further, decreed that the Bethlehem Chapel, "a nest of heretics," should be torn down to its foundations."[19] To relieve Prague of the impact of the interdict and bull against him, Hus left the city near the end of 1412.

For his own safety, Hus moved from place-to-place, preaching and encouraging the saints, finding refuge in the homes of some powerful friends. He wrote a lot of what we now know as Hus' writings during this time. "His treatise on the Church (*De Ecclesia*), written during this period, is the most elaborate and systematic of his Latin works. ... It was from this work mainly that his enemies drew material for their charges against him. ... A Roman Catholic writer of the time, grasping the full bearing of its argument, admits the marked ability of this production. It reduced the whole cumbrous[20]

---

[17] Schwarze, 69-70
[18] Ibid,76
[19] Ibid
[20] Cumbersome

system of priestly rule to a heap of rubbish. It made the faith that works by love, not organic connection with the priest-controlled Romish body, the condition of membership in the spiritual Church of Christ. It made all human distinctions of rank shrink to insignificance before the ennobling relation which the humblest member of the Church sustains to Christ, its head."[21] John Hus was determined to write mostly in his native language, to make his work available to the common people. "What Luther did for the German, Calvin for the French, Hus succeeded in doing for the Bohemian. Each was the father of his native tongue in its modern form."[22]

Time was winding down for the Bohemian; a council had been called to meet in Constance, on the Bodensee in Germany in December of 1414; it lasted nearly four years. The pope, the emperor, thirty cardinals, thirty-three archbishops, 150 bishops, several hundred theological doctors, 4,000 priests, twenty-four princes and dukes, seventy-eight counts, and more than 600 barons gathered for this biggest and more imposing assembly of the Middle Ages. To this assembly, Hus was summoned, his trip paid for by wealthy friends. A few days after his arrival, Hus was arrested and taken to the episcopal palace where cardinals were waiting for him. Hus "wished to be convinced by reason and the Scriptures, not to bow blindly to the authority of the pope or cardinals or council." [23] Hus was moved from one place to another, never to be free on this earth again. He spent over 2 months in a vile prison, his friends

---

[21] Schwarze, 86
[22] Ibid, 96
[23] Ibid, 107

working in vain to free him. Around this time, John XXIII had worn out his welcome in his own religion and he was asked to step down. He ran off to escape punishment, unrepentant for the evil he had done.

History provides us a touch of irony that we cannot pass up. While Hus was in the foul prison in Castle Gottlieben on the Rhine, the man termed anti-pope was captured and thrown into the same prison. Pope John had been convicted by the council on fifty-four charges and judged by it to be "the mirror of infamy, an idolater of the flesh and one whom all who knew him considered a devil incarnate."[24] This "devil incarnate" was released and made peace with the new pope. "Hus, on the contrary, was acknowledged even by his enemies to be a man illustrious for his purity of life. But he dared to think for himself."[25] Standing upon the Word of God and refusing to accept a higher authority as demanded by the Roman priesthood, Hus was despised by that entire power structure. The most dangerous activity in a totalitarian society is thinking. The religion of the world requires submission; the gift of God is liberty that no man can take away.

Hus' temporal freedom was contingent on his acceptance of the supremacy of the Council of Cardinals in all matter of faith. "This Hus could not do, but he again expressed himself as willing to amend his teaching wherever it had been shown to be false, according to the Scriptures."[26] Man cannot bind the conscience of another man; God alone can do this.

---

[24] Schwarze, 117
[25] Ibid
[26] Ibid, 124

Saints are held captive to the Word of God and need not fear man, who can do no more than kill the body.

The trial was a mockery of justice, as is often the case when power-mad rulers demand their way. Hus was not allowed to answer the charges made against him. "The writings of Hus, both in the Latin and Bohemian tongues, were to be committed to the flames. Hus himself was declared to be a true and manifest heretic, who was to be delivered over to the secular authorities for punishment. He knelt and prayed with a loud voice, "Lord Jesus, forgive mine enemies! Thou knowest that they have borne false witness against me. Forgive them for Thy mercy's sake!" At this prayer, many bishops frowned and a mocking laugh burst from their lips."[27]

On the same day, July 6th, 1415, John Hus was burned at the stake, by those who had made friends with the "devil incarnate." Hus' last testimony of the truth that would not let him go was spoken as the wood was piled up around him. ""What shall I recant, not being conscious of any errors I call God to witness that I have neither taught nor preached what has falsely been laid to my charge, but that the end of all my preaching and writings was to induce my fellow men to forsake sin. In the truth which I have proclaimed, according to the Gospel of Jesus Christ and the expositions of holy teachers, I will, this day, joyfully die," At these words the nobles clapped their hands. It was the signal for the execution. The torch was applied."[28] A man who had been used to bring much light to a dark land lit up the

---

[27] Schwarze, 132-133
[28] Ibid, 134-135

sky as darkness killed the body – having no ability to reach his soul.

The people in Bohemia were outraged and much commotion consumed the nation for four years. Some disciples of Hus adopted the name "Unity of the Brethren" (Unitas Fratrum) and, in 1467, gained the friendship of the Waldenses. "Four principles were adopted by the members of the Unitas Fratrum as the basis of their union.

(1) The Bible is the only source of Christian doctrine.

(2) Public worship is to be conducted in accordance with Scripture teaching and on the model of the Apostolic Church.

(3) The Lord's Supper is to be received in faith, to be doctrinally defined in the language of Scripture and every authoritative human explanation of that language is to be avoided.

(4) Godly Christian life is essential as an evidence of saving faith."[29]

By the time of Martin Luther, the Union had 200,000 members; they practiced evangelism and developed an educational program to ward off ignorance. "The Unitas Fratrum enjoys the distinction of having been the first church ever to put a hymn-book into the hands of the people. The first edition bears the date 1501. A single

---

[29] Schwarze, 148

copy of that edition is preserved in the library of the modern University of Prague."[30]

In talking about the early work of the Reformation in Germany, D'Aubigne remarked, "A triple aristocracy – the superior clergy, the nobles, and the university – check the free expansion of Christian convictions."[31] These tendencies of natural man, clawing for power and prestige, always work against the people of God; but God cannot be defeated. With increasing clarity, yet still through a glass dimly, the early Reformers emerged from providential darkness into the growing light of grace.

"The Renaissance" was "the name given to that revival of interest in Art and Classical literature which swept across Europe during the fourteenth century."[32] Much of this was fueled by the exodus of scholars who fled the conquering Turks, "bringing with them the influence of their own learning and many, priceless Greek manuscripts. ... A new age was dawning, an age of enquiry, adventure and a thirst for learning. ... In the production of the Bible, whereas the copies of Wycliffe's translation had to be written out laboriously by hand, it was now possible to produce them in thousands. ... It broke men loose from the fetters with which the Roman Church had bound their minds, and there was kindled a new spirit of investigation into the meaning of the Word of God which was carried back

---

[30] Schwarze, 149
[31] J.H. Merle D'Aubigne, *History of the Reformation*, Volume Four, Book XIII, page 307
[32] Kennedy, 131

beyond the imperfections of the Latin Vulgate to the original sources."[33]

Erasmus arose as another subject of Rome who was given light to see her errors. He "advocated the translation of the Scriptures into the common tongues. He also freely used his wit and gift of expression to criticize and satirise the superstition and error of the Church. ... Erasmus was too clear sighted a man not to be aware of the evils of Rome, and many of his writings were directed towards a change from within, but he was too much the passive scholar to go to the lengths of breaking with the Church he criticized. ... The Greek New Testament renewed the emphasis made by Wycliffe and others on the pre-eminence of the authority of the Word of God, and at the same time opened up the way to a clearer understanding of its contents. The Word of God made plain opened the way for a fresh expression of the life of Christ in His people gathered together in His name."[34]

As with others, Erasmus' life shows us how large institutions are most difficult to change; but change is normal in the context of institutional entropy, as they "degenerate to the purely human. Rome has certainly changed with the times, but the direction of its move has not been towards the simplicity of the early churches. And the same is true of the great communions of that section of Christendom that is now called Protestant. Change there has been, but always is has been towards the dominance of man, not of God. ... In every age God has had afresh to gather out a people unto Himself. He is still doing it."[35] This should be a warning to all of us to resist the siren call of pragmatism, "doing ministry" to get the results we want. Our call – the call to every child of God – is to be faithful with what we've each been given, to bear in mind it is His gospel that will soften hearts as the Holy Spirit does what no man can do. We must water and plant but must ever be mindful that he who waters and he who plants is nothing. God gives the increase – brings new life – and He is everything.

Another name emerges from this era. William Tyndale studied at Oxford alongside of Erasmus. "It was Oxford, where Erasmus was so well known, that received his Greek Testament so warmly, and it was there that Tyndale, in his study of this much discussed book, felt the full impact of the Word of God upon his life."[36] Erasmus quickly developed a group of friends to read his Greek New Testament. "The clergy began to grow alarmed at the threat to their authority posed by those who were beginning to recognize the authority of God revealed directly through His Word, and Tyndale left Oxford for Cambridge."[37] God used this to fan the flames of His witness in Cambridge.

A Roman Cardinal, Wolsey, was a papal legate who had eyes on the papacy, "so it well suited his purpose to become the great champion of Catholic orthodoxy and the Church's stalwart defender against the 'pernicious heresy' of the Bible."[38] Tyndale left Cambridge and

---

[35] Kennedy, 133
[36] Ibid
[37] Ibid
[38] Ibid, 134

found refuge in the home of Sir John Walsh, who hired him as a tutor to their children. He brought current events into the lessons, "the New Learning, Luther, Erasmus and the Scriptures. Tyndale took his full share in the animated repartee, and substantiated his points by reference to the Greek New Testament, a copy of which he always kept at hand."[39] He continued to draw the ire of the Roman clergy, most of whom were so ignorant of the Scriptures, made all the more evident by Tyndale's "avid mind and ever-ready reply from the Word of God to priestly superstitions. Tyndale was shocked to realize how ignorant the clergy were of the Bible, but it spurred him on to the momentous decision that his life would be devoted to giving to the people of England God's Word in their own language."[40] Attributed to Tyndale is the sentiment that a plowboy with the Bible would be more learned, educated, than the King. "To pursue his God-given task, Tyndale had to flee his own country when only about thirty years of age. ... He lived his life as a hunted man."[41]

Think about that: because he believed the Bible, Tyndale was hunted by the state-church, unable to live a normal life – no family, no sense of belonging, always on the move, looking over his shoulder. Satisfied to be hated by the world and approved by the Creator.

The first edition of his English New Testament was produced in 1526 and copies were smuggled into England. "In 1536 at Vilvorde near Brussels he was led from his prison to the place of execution. Chained to a

---

[39] Kennedy, 134
[40] Ibid
[41] Ibid

massive wooden cross with a noose around his neck, the faggots were piled around his body. ... fire was struck ... and the unassuming body that housed so great a soul was reduced to ashes."[42]

> While Tyndale was living out the last years of his life on the Continent of Europe, the tide of events was moving swiftly in England. Henry VIII, furious with the Pope's duplicity in failing to order affairs to suit his amorous designs, finally severed the connection of England with the Roman Church by the passing, in 1534, of the Supremacy Act which declared the king to be the 'Supreme Head of the Church of England.' The ban on the English Bible was relaxed, for a little while at least, and Miles Coverdale produced, in 1535 the first, complete printed versions of the Scriptures in English, basing his translation on Tyndale's great work on the New Testament and part of the Old. Coverdale's Bible was the first to circulate freely in England and was doing so while Tyndale was dying a martyr's death at Vilvorde.[43]

As previously mentioned, many men used of God were forgotten while some who came later were memorialized for far less sacrifice. So it has been with King Henry the 8th of England.

> Henry VIII has been called the 'father of the English Reformation'. That may be so if what is meant by the Reformation is simply the severing

---

of the religious tie between England and Rome, but the fat, licentious monarch who so readily sacrificed his wives and subjects, Protestants and Catholics alike, to gratify his every regal whim, was certainly not the father of that spiritual movement whereby men and women, regenerated by the power of a risen Christ, were free to meet around their Lord and display to the world the testimony of a glorified Saviour in the church. Spiritual reformation is based upon more solid ground, the ground of the Word of God which liveth and abideth forever. ... this foundation and the church built upon it, as we have seen, has never been absent from the world since the church was first established at Pentecost, in spite of all the attempts of the arch-enemy to overthrow it. And the advent of the Reformation era was to bring with it its own subtle attacks upon the testimony of the living church.[44]

The Dark Ages came to end when the light of the gospel of Christ Jesus burst forth as God called papal monks out of the darkness of that cult. As Kennedy reminds us, "the center of everything meaningful about the Reformation is a Book, not a man or men. ... Our history ... is mainly concerned with ... the tracing of the spiritual history of the spiritual church through the ages."[45]

I thank God for the Reformation but urge us not to lose sight of the One Who caused all these things to work together to good for those who are called by His name.

---

[44] Kennedy, 136
[45] Ibid, 137

All throughout the age, from time of Paul and John up until even now, YHWH has preserved a remnant of His people in each generation. He brought myriad circumstances together in the 16th century and we have GREATLY benefited from His kindness. The GOOD that came out of the reformation is the handiwork of God - let all the saints praise Him! But such activity is not the focus of His redemptive plan any more than national Israel was. The culmination of all of Scripture settles on the person and finished work of the Lord Jesus. Our attention must remain on Christ and not mere men or events in history.

In any situation, even the redeemed are vulnerable to being pulled aside by myriad temptations. Ulrich Zwingli serves as an example and warning for us. He was educated at the University of Vienna and began teaching in 1506, being later appointed to preach by Zurich Council which was legally responsible for civil and religious order. "In 1520 the council issued an order that all pastors and preachers should declare the pure word of God, and Zwingli had announced as his principle the rejection of everything in doctrine or practice not warranted by the Scriptures."[46] This order was renewed in 1523 after Zwingli had a public dispute with papists. "At the outset Zwingli had been intimate with the people who later opened the Second Front. He had, in fact, to quite an extent shared their views, a fact to which the Stepchildren were not slow to point. He had, for example, said that infant baptism "nit sin solle," ought not to be."[47] These "Second Front" people were

---

[46] Vedder, *A Short History of the Baptists*, 55
[47] Leonard Verduin, *Reformers and Their Stepchildren*, page 38

Anabaptists (as were all "heretics" who refused to submit to Rome) later known as the Swiss Brethren, one of whom said to Zwingli, "You have no business giving these decisions into the hands of the civil power."[48] It was this point that the lines between the Reformers and their Stepchildren began to emerge.

Zwingli found himself pulled by the Anabaptists to be faithful to his pledge to renounce "everything in doctrine or practice not warranted by the Scriptures" on the one hand and the long-standing tradition of the state-church on the other. "He was in bondage to the idea of a State Church, a reformation that should have back of it the power of the civil magistrate, instead of being a spiritual movement simply. But to fulfil this ideal, infant baptism was a necessity. The moment the church was made a body consisting wholly of the regenerate, it of necessity separated itself from the world. The Zurich Council had supported the reform thus far, but by no means all its members—possibly not the majority— were regenerate men. How far would they support a reform that would, as a first step, unchurch them and deprive their children of the privilege (as they still esteemed it) of baptism? Such a policy of reform seemed to Zwingli suicide at the very beginning, for he could see a possibility of success only through the support of the civil power."[49]

Zwingli realized that disciples' baptism is what Scripture teaches, yet he saw this practice as a danger to the state-church which provided his livelihood. "So Zwingli retained infant baptism, but without rationale

---

[48] Verduin, 38
[49] Vedder, *A Short History of the Baptists*, 56

for it. What could he do? Faced with these hard choices, he adopted "a completely new hermeneutical approach to Scripture as a whole, i.e., the idea of the unity of the covenant of grace." Other Reformed writers followed his example when contending against the Anabaptists."[50] This was the foundation for what later became the Westminster system of theology; a complex systematic theology built around the idea of protecting infant baptism, so-called, undergirded by the over-arching covenant of grace. "This was a doctrine forged in the heat of the Anabaptist controversy in the summer of 1525. It was first used to bolster the argument for infant baptism in Zwingli's "Reply to Humaier" in November of that year."[51] Zwingli reminds us that self-deception is the most dangerous, as it's the most difficult to discern and the most demanding of one's loyalty.

In January of 1525 the Zurich Council, with Zwingli in the lead, "issued an order that parents should have their children baptized at once, on pain of banishment. ... On March 7, 1526, it was decreed by the Zurich Council that whosoever rebaptized should be drowned, and this action was confirmed by a second decree of November 19. Felix Mantz, who had been released for a time and had renewed his labors at Schaffhausen and Basel, was rearrested on December 3, found guilty of the heinous crime of Anabaptism, and on January 5 was sentenced to death by drowning."[52]

---

[50] Tom Well & Fred Zaspell, *New Covenant Theology*, page 3
[51] Jack Cottrell, *Baptism: Zwingli or the Bible?*, page 32
[52] Vedder, *A Short History of the Baptists,* 56-57

The teachings of the Swiss Anabaptists are accurately known to us from three independent and mutually confirmatory sources: The testimony of their opponents, the fragments of their writings that remain, and their Confession of Faith. The latter is the first document of its kind known to be in existence. It was issued in 1527 by the "brotherly union of certain believing, baptized children of God," assembled at Schleitheim, a little village near Schaffhausen. The author is conjectured to have been Michael Sattler, of whom we know little more than that he was an ex-monk, of highly esteemed character, who suffered martyrdom at Rothenberg in the same year this confession was issued, his tongue being torn out, his body lacerated with red-hot tongs, and then burned.[53]

Coercion is ever the modus operandi of the state-church. When religion is wed to politics, the power to tax leads to the use of force, as non-conformance to the state religion is not permissible. This rails against the theology of the Kingdom of God revealed by the Lord Jesus, which is not of this world (John 18:36) but exists in this world in the hearts of His people.

About this, last apostle expounded in some detail:

Now I, Paul, make a personal appeal to you by the gentleness and graciousness of Christ *— I who am humble among you in person but bold toward you when absent. I beg you that when I am present I will not need to be bold with the confidence by which I plan to*

---

*challenge certain people who think we are behaving in an unspiritual way. **For though we live in the body, we do not wage war in an unspiritual way**, since the weapons of our warfare are not worldly, but are powerful through God for the demolition of strongholds. We demolish arguments and every high-minded thing that is raised up against the knowledge of God, taking every thought captive to obey Christ.* (2 Cor. 10:1-5)

Mental and physical coercion are carnal, fleshly, demonic, worldly weapons. Their use has no place within the Kingdom of God[54]. This conflation of these two realms has been the sad legacy of many who sought to break from Rome, but brought much of that cult's ways into their own teaching and doctrine.

In the late 19th century, the renowned church historian Phillip Schaff wrote a letter to a friend, Dr. Mann of Germany, in which he observed:

> The Reformation everywhere had its defects and sins, which it is impossible to justify. How cruel was the persecution of the Anabaptists, who by no means were only revolutionary fanatics but for the most part simple, honest Christians and suffered and died for liberty of conscience and the separation of church and state. And how sad were the moral state and the rude theological quarrels in Germany. No wonder that Melanchthon longed for deliverance from the rabies theologorum[55]. I hope God has something

---

[54] James 3:13-18
[55] ED: "rabies theologorum" means "madness of the theologians."

better and greater in store for His Church than the Reformation.[56]

On this matter of using the state as an agent of the church (as taught by the original Westminster Confession of Faith) to coerce proper "Christian" behavior, Baptists stand apart from our Reformed brothers and sisters. We would rather identify with the saints of old who were described in *Epistola ad Diognetum* in the early part of the second century:

> The Christians are not distinguished from other men by country, by language, nor by civil institutions. For they neither dwell in cities by themselves, nor use a peculiar tongue, nor lead a singular mode of life. They dwell in the Grecian or barbarian cities, as the case may be; they follow the usages of the country in dress, food, and the other affairs of life. Yet they present a wonderful and confessedly paradoxical conduct They dwell in their own native lands, but as strangers. They take part in all things, as citizens; and they suffer all things, as foreigners. Every foreign country is a fatherland to them, and every native land is a foreign. They marry, like all others; they have children; but they do not cast away their offsprings. They have the table in common, but not wives. They are in the flesh, but do not live after the flesh. They live upon the earth, but are citizens of heaven. They obey the existing laws, and excel the laws by their lives. They love all, and are persecuted by all. They are unknown, and yet they are condemned. They are

---

[56] David S. Schaff, *The Life of Phillip Schaff*, page 462

killed and made alive. They are poor and make many rich. They lack all things, and in all things abound. They are reproached, and glory in their reproaches. They are calumniated, and are justified. They are cursed, and they bless. They receive scorn, and they give honor. They do good and are punished as evil-doers. When punished, they rejoice, as being made alive. By the Jews they are attacked as aliens, and by the Greeks persecuted; and the cause of the enmity their enemies cannot tell. In short, what the soul is to the body, the Christians are in the world. The soul is diffused through all the members of the body, and the Christians are spread through the cities of the world. The soul dwells in the body, but it is not of the body; so the Christians dwell in the world, but are not of the world. The soul, invisible, keeps watch in the visible body; so also the Christians are seen to live in the world, for their piety is invisible. The flesh hates and wars against the soul; suffering no wrong from it, but because it resists fleshly pleasures; and the world hates the Christians with no reason, but they resist its pleasures. The soul loves the flesh and members, by which it is hated; so the Christians love their haters. The soul is enclosed in the body, but holds the body together; so the Christians are detained in the world as in a prison; but they contain the world. Immortal, the soul dwells in the mortal body; so the Christians dwell in the corruptible, but look for incorruption in heaven. The soul is the better for restriction in food and drink; and the Christians increase, though daily punished. This lot God has assigned to the Christians in the world; and it cannot be taken from them.[57]

Does this not ring with the truth of Scripture in a way the carnage of the state-church cannot? Dear reader, does your soul rejoice in knowing you have security in Christ the world cannot destroy? Do you yearn to be completely free from sin and want to live your remaining days for His glory? Such desires are the work of the Holy Spirit in His people.

May God keep us from being led astray by false teaching which appeals to our flesh but does not line up with Scripture.

2 Corinthians 4:6 *For God who said, "Let light shine out of darkness," has shone in our hearts to give the light of the knowledge of God's glory in the face of Jesus Christ.*

---

[57] Christian, 12, 13

In Darkness – Light!

Conclusion

John 1:1-5 *In the beginning was the Word, and the Word was with God, and the Word was God. He was with God in the beginning. All things were created through Him, and apart from Him not one thing was created that has been created. Life was in Him, and that life was the light of men. That light shines in the darkness, yet the darkness did not overcome it.*

A thousand years had passed. Satan and countless of his minions had harassed, persecuted, tortured, and murdered countless (the number known to God) children of the most high God. Families had been torn apart, the Bible kept in dead languages, people kept in ignorance.

But God.

Just as He showed Elijah that He had 7,000 who had not bowed the knee to Baal, so He reminds us that if He is with us, who can be against us? (Romans 8:31) One man I have not spent time on this book comes to us now. As the Lord of light began to push back the spiritual darkness that had tormented men for a millennium, Martin Luther wrote a hymn that is a most fitting victory song for all who love the Lord Jesus and await His return, not to deal with sin but to gather all who eagerly look for Him. He is our fortress!

> A mighty Fortress is our God
> A Bulwark never failing
> Our Helper He amid the flood
> Of mortal ills prevailing

For still our ancient foe
Doth seek to work us woe
His craft and power are great
And, armed with cruel hate
On earth is not his equal

Did we in our own strength confide
Our striving would be losing
Were not the right Man on our side
The Man of God's own choosing

Dost ask who that may be?
Christ Jesus, it is He
Lord Sabaoth His Name
From age to age, the same
And He must win the battle

And though this world, with devils filled
Should threaten to undo us
We will not fear, for God hath willed
His truth to triumph through us

The Prince of Darkness grim
We tremble not for him
His rage we can endure
For lo, his doom is sure
One little word shall fell him

That word above all earthly powers
No, thanks to them, abideth
The Spirit and the gifts are ours
Through Him who with us sideth

> Let goods and kindred go
> This mortal life also
> The body they may kill
> God's truth abideth still
> His Kingdom is forever

I marvel that this hymn, written in German, comes across in English this powerfully! With this God on our side, we cannot lose! God is on our side only if He has chosen us to be on His. *All things are from Him and through Him and to Him are all things. To Him be the glory forever. Amen.* (Romans 11:36)

For this reason, the way we read the Bible needs to be oriented toward Him. The Bible is best seen as a large-scale story of God's redemptive plan, with the providential hand of God behind all. Post-biblical history has the same scheme, without the inspiration of God behind the words written. As He steered the events leading up to the birth and sacrificial death of Christ, so He steers human history towards its climax when Christ Jesus returns. The gospel of salvation from sin is not complete without the recognition that this same gospel includes His second advent and all the redeemed being raised up in glorified bodies to dwell with Him on the new earth. In this, we receive the ultimate goodness from God that is possible for creatures – a glory that angels marvel at. They have not been forgiven, have not the experience of redemption. This is the culmination of Romans 8:28 – God having worked out ALL things for our good, those are have been called by Him and love Him.

History is largely written by the victors. During the prelude before the dark ages, the rising influence of the

Roman Catholic Church had given it victor status in several countries on the European Continent and not until the invention of the printing press did the non-conformists have the tools to put their theology before the people. The final chapter of history is yet to written, though the outcome has been determined. The ultimate victor has told us outcome:

> *In the days of those kings, the God of heaven will set up a kingdom that will never be destroyed, and this kingdom will not be left to another people. It will crush all these kingdoms and bring them to an end, but will itself endure forever. You saw a stone break off from the mountain without a hand touching it, and it crushed the iron, bronze, fired clay, silver, and gold. The great God has told the king what will happen in the future. The dream is true, and its interpretation certain.* (Dan 2:44-45)

Providence has been described as God's control over happenstance. As Jesus said, this is God's doing and it is marvelous in your eyes!

In the Scriptures, as well as in more recent history, we tend to focus on our heroes and make much of them. I heard Paul Washer at a conference one time stop in the middle of his message and declare, "I am sick and tired of hearing about "great men of God!" There are no great men of God! There are sinful men used by a great and mighty God!" Let this be our focus as we see how history – His story – unfolded since Scripture closed.

Any religion that has priests as officers within is not a Christian religion. A priest is a man who stands between the people and their god. In the Christian faith, all the redeemed are priests and kings unto our God and there is no mediator between God and man except for Jesus the God-man.

Stephen Wellum observed that Anselm had failed to make clear how the cross of Christ is appropriated by us. "Into this silence, Thomas Aquinas (1224-1274) spoke. As Gwenfair Walters notes, Aquinas made more explicit the relationship between Christ's cross and our appropriation of it via the sacraments as mediated by the church. As Aquinas made clear:

> Christ's Passion is the sufficient cause of man's salvation. But it does not follow that the sacraments are not also necessary for that purpose: because they obtain their effect through the power of Christ's Passion; and Christ's Passion is, so to say, applied to man through the sacraments according to the Apostle Paul (Rom. 4:3); *All we who are baptized in Christ Jesus, are baptized into His death.*

"As this developed in medieval theology, the sacraments were *necessary* for salvation because it was through them that Christ's atonement was applied to us and we are made righteous. ... The grace that is communicated through the sacraments is infused so that our nature is transformed, and by this infusion, we are enabled to cooperate with God to merit eternal life."[1]

This is why the governing category of all Christian theology is the Creator-creature

---

[1] Stephen Wellum, *Christ Alone, the Uniqueness of Jesus as Savior*, pages 171, 172.

distinction: God alone is God, and all else depends upon him for its existence.[2]

What Rome missed is "the central theological insight of the Reformation, namely that the triune, self-sufficient God *cannot* forgive our sin without satisfaction of his own righteous moral demand."[3] Men who are not satisfied with forgiveness according to grace will always add their own works to the equation, for natural man is hard-wired for works righteousness. This is the siren call of the world's religion, the damning error of thinking Christ is not enough.

What Rome continues to miss, what every false religion continues to miss is the biblical truth that peace with God can only be found by grace alone, through faith alone, in Christ Jesus alone. While the world and all its devilish hoards rail against us, our anchor holds, Christ is a sure refuge in time of storm.

> Should seven storms of vengeance roll
> And shake this earth from pole to pole
> No thunderbolt shall daunt my face
> While Jesus is my hiding place
>
> On Him almighty vengeance fell
> Which would have sunk this world to Hell
> He bore it for a sinful race
> To make Himself our hiding place[4]

---

[2] Wellum, 177.
[3] Ibid, 180.
[4] Matthew Smith, Hiding Place

May the Word of God dwell richly in our minds, as we fix our eyes on what is unseen, the heavenlies from where our help comes.

So if you have been raised with the Messiah, seek what is above, where the Messiah is, seated at the right hand of God. Set your minds on what is above, not on what is on the earth. For you have died, and your life is hidden with the Messiah in God. When the Messiah, who is your life, is revealed, then you also will be revealed with Him in glory. (Colossians 3:1 - 4)

Cry out to Him in time of trouble and in time of peace, the Lord is close to His own and will never abandon us.

God, hear my cry; pay attention to my prayer. I call to You from the ends of the earth when my heart is without strength. Lead me to a rock that is high above me, for You have been a refuge for me, a strong tower in the face of the enemy. I will live in Your tent forever and take refuge under the shelter of Your wings. Selah (Psalm 61:1 – 4)

Psalm 112:4 *Light shines in the darkness for the upright. He is gracious, compassionate, and righteous.*

Post Script

Dear reader, please seek comfort from God in every trial and success. Look to His written record to find this comfort, that His Spirit will confirm in your soul. John's Apocalypse/The Revelation of Christ is intended by our God to be a major source of comfort to His frail children as we face countless trials and much tribulation. Christ

Jesus is our refuge, our wisdom, our intercessor, our judge, and our elder brother. There is no more sure refuge than having faith in Christ.

Behold our God, seated on His throne. Come! Let us adore Him! Behold our King! Nothing can compare! Come! Let us adore Him![5]

When He took the scroll, the four living creatures and the 24 elders fell down before the Lamb. Each one had a harp and gold bowls filled with incense, which are the prayers of the saints. And they sang a new song:

> *You are worthy to take the scroll and to open its seals, because* **You were slaughtered, and You redeemed people for God by Your blood from every tribe and language and people and nation. You made them a kingdom and priests to our God, and they will reign on the earth.**

Then I looked and heard the voice of many angels around the throne, and also of the living creatures and of the elders. Their number was countless thousands, plus thousands of thousands. They said with a loud voice:

> **The Lamb who was slaughtered is worthy to receive power and riches and wisdom and strength and honor and glory and blessing!**

I heard every creature in heaven, on earth, under the earth, on the sea, and everything in them say:

---

[5] Sovereign Grace Music, Behold Our God.

Blessing and honor and glory and dominion to the One seated on the throne, and to the Lamb, forever and ever!

The four living creatures said, "Amen," and the elders fell down and worshiped.

Revelation 5:8-14

"Look! I am coming quickly, and My reward is with Me to repay each person according to what he has done. I am the Alpha and the Omega, the First and the Last, the Beginning and the End.

"Blessed are those who wash their robes, so that they may have the right to the tree of life and may enter the city by the gates. Outside are the dogs, the sorcerers, the sexually immoral, the murderers, the idolaters, and everyone who loves and practices lying.

"I, Jesus, have sent My angel to attest these things to you for the churches. I am the Root and the Offspring of David, the Bright Morning Star." Both the Spirit and the bride say, "Come!" Anyone who hears should say, "Come!" And the one who is thirsty should come. Whoever desires should take the living water as a gift.

Revelation 22:12-17

FINIS!

159

In Darkness – Light!

Appendix 1: Early Creeds

Apostles' Creed

I believe in God the Father Almighty, Maker of heaven and earth.

And in Jesus Christ his only Son our Lord; who was conceived by the Holy Ghost, born of the Virgin Mary, suffered under Pontius Pilate, was crucified, dead, and buried; he descended into hell; the third day he rose again from the dead; he ascended into heaven, and sitteth on the right hand of God the Father Almighty; from thence he shall come to judge the quick and the dead.

I believe in the Holy Ghost; the holy catholic Church; the communion of saints; the forgiveness of sins; the resurrection of the body; and the life everlasting. AMEN.

The Creed of Nicaea, approved by the First Ecumenical Council (A.D. 325)

We believe in one God, the Father, the Almighty, maker of heaven and earth, of all that is, seen and unseen.

We believe in one Lord, Jesus Christ, the only Son of God, eternally begotten of the Father, God from God, Light from Light, true God from true God, begotten, not made, of one Being with the Father. Through him all things were made. For us and for our salvation he came down from heaven: by the power of the Holy Spirit he became incarnate from the Virgin Mary, and was made man. For our sake he was crucified under Pontius Pilate; he suffered death and was buried. On the third day, he rose again in accordance with the Scriptures; he ascended into heaven and is seated at the right hand of the Father. He will come again in glory to judge the living and the dead, and his kingdom will have no end.

We believe in the Holy Spirit, the Lord, the giver of life, who proceeds from the Father. With the Father and the Son he is worshiped and glorified. He has spoken through the Prophets. We believe in one holy catholic and apostolic Church. We acknowledge one baptism for the forgiveness of sins. We look for the resurrection of the dead, and the life of the world to come. Amen.

The Nicene Creed, as approved by the First Council of Constantinople (A.D. 381)

I believe in one God, the Father almighty, maker of heaven and earth, of all things visible and invisible.

I believe in one Lord Jesus Christ, the Only Begotten Son of God, born of the Father before all ages. God from God, Light from Light, true God from true God, begotten, not made, consubstantial with the Father; through him all things were made.

For us men and for our salvation he came down from heaven, and by the Holy Spirit was incarnate of the Virgin Mary, and became man.

For our sake he was crucified under Pontius Pilate, he suffered death and was buried, and rose again on the third day in accordance with the Scriptures. He ascended into heaven and is seated at the right hand of the Father.

He will come again in glory to judge the living and the dead and his kingdom will have no end.

I believe in the Holy Spirit, the Lord, the giver of life, who proceeds from the Father and the Son, who with the Father and the Son is adored and glorified, who has spoken through the prophets.

I believe in one, holy, catholic and apostolic Church.

I confess one Baptism for the forgiveness of sins and I look forward to the resurrection of the dead and the life of the world to come. Amen.

Definition of Chalcedon (A.D. 451)

Following, then, the holy fathers, we unite in teaching all men to confess the one and only Son, our Lord Jesus Christ. This selfsame one is perfect both in deity and in humanness; this selfsame one is also actually God and actually man, with a rational soul {meaning human soul} and a body. He is of the same reality as God as far as his deity is concerned and of the same reality as we ourselves as far as his humanness is concerned; thus like us in all respects, sin only excepted. Before time began he was begotten of the Father, in respect of his deity, and now in these "last days," for us and behalf of our salvation, this selfsame one was born of Mary the virgin, who is God-bearer in respect of his humanness.

We also teach that we apprehend this one and only Christ-Son, Lord, only-begotten -- in two natures; and we do this without confusing the two natures, without transmuting one nature into the other, without dividing them into two separate categories, without contrasting them according to area or function. The distinctiveness of each nature is not nullified by the union. Instead, the "properties" of each nature are conserved and both natures concur in one "person" and in one reality {hypostasis}. They are not divided or cut into two persons, but are together the one and only and only-begotten Word {Logos} of God, the Lord Jesus Christ. Thus have the prophets of old testified; thus the Lord Jesus Christ himself taught us; thus the Symbol of Fathers {the Nicene Creed} has handed down to us.

Council of Orange (A.D. 529)

CANON 1. If anyone denies that it is the whole man, that is, both body and soul, that was "changed for the worse" through the offense of Adam's sin, but believes that the freedom of the soul remains unimpaired and that only the body is subject to corruption, he is deceived by the error of Pelagius and contradicts the scripture which says, "The soul that sins shall die" (Ezek. 18:20); and, "Do you not know that if you yield yourselves to anyone as obedient slaves, you are the slaves of the one whom you obey?" (Rom. 6:16); and, "For whatever overcomes a man, to that he is enslaved" (2 Pet. 2:19).

CANON 2. If anyone asserts that Adam's sin affected him alone and not his descendants also, or at least if he declares that it is only the death of the body which is the punishment for sin, and not also that sin, which is the death of the soul, passed through one man to the whole human race, he does injustice to God and contradicts the Apostle, who says, "Therefore as sin came into the world through one man and death through sin, and so death spread to all men because all men sinned" (Rom. 5:12).

CANON 3. If anyone says that the grace of God can be conferred as a result of human prayer, but that it is not grace itself which makes us pray to God, he contradicts the prophet Isaiah, or the Apostle who says the same thing, "I have been found by those who did not seek me; I have shown myself to those who did not ask for me" (Rom 10:20, quoting Isa. 65:1).

CANON 4. If anyone maintains that God awaits our will to be cleansed from sin, but does not confess that even our will to be cleansed comes to us through the infusion and working of the Holy Spirit, he resists the Holy Spirit himself who says through Solomon, "The will is prepared by the Lord" (Prov. 8:35, LXX), and the salutary word of the Apostle, "For God is at work in you, both to will and to work for his good pleasure" (Phil. 2:13).

CANON 5. If anyone says that not only the increase of faith but also its beginning and the very desire for faith, by which we believe in Him who justifies the ungodly and comes to the regeneration of holy baptism -- if anyone says that this belongs to us by nature and not by a gift of grace, that is, by the inspiration of the Holy Spirit amending our will and turning it from unbelief to faith and from godlessness to godliness, it is proof that he is opposed to the teaching of the Apostles, for blessed Paul says, "And I am sure that he who began a good work in you will bring it to completion at the day of

Jesus Christ" (Phil. 1:6). And again, "For by grace you have been saved through faith; and this is not your own doing, it is the gift of God" (Eph. 2:8). For those who state that the faith by which we believe in God is natural make all who are separated from the Church of Christ by definition in some measure believers.

CANON 6. If anyone says that God has mercy upon us when, apart from his grace, we believe, will, desire, strive, labor, pray, watch, study, seek, ask, or knock, but does not confess that it is by the infusion and inspiration of the Holy Spirit within us that we have the faith, the will, or the strength to do all these things as we ought; or if anyone makes the assistance of grace depend on the humility or obedience of man and does not agree that it is a gift of grace itself that we are obedient and humble, he contradicts the Apostle who says, "What have you that you did not receive?" (1 Cor. 4:7), and, "But by the grace of God I am what I am" (1 Cor. 15:10).

CANON 7. If anyone affirms that we can form any right opinion or make any right choice which relates to the salvation of eternal life, as is expedient for us, or that we can be saved, that is, assent to the preaching of the gospel through our natural powers without the illumination and inspiration of the Holy Spirit, who makes all men gladly assent to and believe in the truth, he is led astray by a heretical spirit, and does not understand the voice of God who says in the Gospel, "For apart from me you can do nothing" (John 15:5), and the word of the Apostle, "Not that we are competent of ourselves to claim anything as coming from us; our competence is from God" (2 Cor. 3:5).

CANON 8. If anyone maintains that some are able to come to the grace of baptism by mercy but others through free will, which has manifestly been corrupted in all those who have been born after the transgression of the first man, it is proof that he has no place in the true faith. For he denies that the free will of all men has been weakened through the sin of the first man, or at least holds that it has been affected in such a way that they have still the ability to seek the mystery of eternal salvation by themselves without the revelation of God. The Lord himself shows how contradictory this is by declaring that no one is able to come to him "unless the Father who sent me draws him" (John 6:44), as he also says to Peter, "Blessed are you, Simon Bar-Jona! For flesh and blood has not revealed this to you, but my Father who is in heaven" (Matt. 16:17), and as the Apostle says, "No one can say 'Jesus is Lord' except by the Holy Spirit" (1 Cor. 12:3).

CANON 9. Concerning the succor of God. It is a mark of divine favor when we are of a right purpose and keep our feet from hypocrisy and unrighteousness; for as often as we do good, God is at work in us and with us, in order that we may do so.

CANON 10. Concerning the succor of God. The succor of God is to be ever sought by the regenerate and converted also, so that they may be able to come to a successful end or persevere in good works.

CANON 11. Concerning the duty to pray. None would make any true prayer to the Lord had he not received from him the object of his prayer, as it is written, "Of thy own have we given thee" (1 Chron. 29:14).

167

CANON 12. Of what sort we are whom God loves. God loves us for what we shall be by his gift, and not by our own deserving.

CANON 13. Concerning the restoration of free will. The freedom of will that was destroyed in the first man can be restored only by the grace of baptism, for what is lost can be returned only by the one who was able to give it. Hence the Truth itself declares: "So if the Son makes you free, you will be free indeed" (John 8:36).

CANON 14. No mean wretch is freed from his sorrowful state, however great it may be, save the one who is anticipated by the mercy of God, as the Psalmist says, "Let thy compassion come speedily to meet us" (Ps. 79:8), and again, "My God in his steadfast love will meet me" (Ps. 59:10).

CANON 15. Adam was changed, but for the worse, through his own iniquity from what God made him. Through the grace of God the believer is changed, but for the better, from what his iniquity has done for him. The one, therefore, was the change brought about by the first sinner; the other, according to the Psalmist, is the change of the right hand of the Most High (Ps. 77:10).

CANON 16. No man shall be honored by his seeming attainment, as though it were not a gift, or suppose that he has received it because a missive from without stated it in writing or in speech. For the Apostle speaks thus, "For if justification were through the law, then Christ died to no purpose" (Gal. 2:21); and "When he ascended on high he led a host of captives, and he gave gifts to men" (Eph. 4:8, quoting Ps. 68:18). It is from this source that any man has what he does; but whoever denies that he has it from this source either does not truly have it, or else "even what he has will be taken away" (Matt. 25:29).

CANON 17. Concerning Christian courage. The courage of the Gentiles is produced by simple greed, but the courage of Christians by the love of God which "has been poured into our hearts" not by freedom of will from our own side but "through the Holy Spirit which has been given to us" (Rom. 5:5).

CANON 18. That grace is not preceded by merit. Recompense is due to good works if they are performed; but grace, to which we have no claim, precedes them, to enable them to be done.

CANON 19. That a man can be saved only when God shows mercy. Human nature, even though it remained in that sound state in which it was created, could be no means save itself, without the assistance of the Creator; hence since man cannot safe- guard his salvation without the grace of God, which is a gift, how will he be able to restore what he has lost without the grace of God?

CANON 20. That a man can do no good without God. God does much that is good in a man that the man does not do; but a man does nothing good for which God is not responsible, so as to let him do it.

CANON 21. Concerning nature and grace. As the Apostle most truly says to those who would be justified by the law and have fallen from grace, "If justification were through the law, then Christ died to no purpose" (Gal. 2:21), so it is most truly declared to those who imagine that grace, which faith in Christ advocates and lays hold of, is nature: "If justification were through nature, then Christ died to no purpose." Now there was indeed the law, but it did not justify, and there was indeed nature, but it did not justify. Not in vain did Christ therefore die, so that the law might be fulfilled by him who said, "I have come not to abolish them but to fulfill them" (Matt. 5:17), and that the nature which had been destroyed by Adam might be restored by him who said that he had come "to seek and to save the lost" (Luke 19:10).

CANON 22. Concerning those things that belong to man. No man has anything of his own but untruth and sin. But if a man has any truth or righteousness, it from that fountain for which we must thirst in this desert, so that we may be refreshed from it as by drops of water and not faint on the way.

CANON 23. Concerning the will of God and of man. Men do their own will and not the will of God when they do what displeases him; but when they follow their own will and comply with the will of God, however willingly they do so, yet it is his will by which what they will is both prepared and instructed.

CANON 24. Concerning the branches of the vine. The branches on the vine do not give life to the vine, but receive life from it; thus the vine is related to its branches in such a way that it supplies them with what they need to live, and does not take this from them. Thus it is to the advantage of the disciples, not Christ, both to have Christ abiding in them and to abide in Christ. For if the vine is cut down another can shoot up from the live root; but one who is cut off from the vine cannot live without the root (John 15:5ff).

CANON 25. Concerning the love with which we love God. It is wholly a gift of God to love God. He who loves, even though he is not loved, allowed himself to be loved. We are loved, even when we displease him, so that we might have means to please him. For the Spirit, whom we love with the Father and the Son, has poured into our hearts the love of the Father and the Son (Rom. 5:5).

CONCLUSION. And thus according to the passages of holy scripture quoted above or the interpretations of the ancient Fathers we must, under the blessing of God, preach and believe as follows. The sin of the first man has so impaired and weakened free will that no one thereafter can either love God as he ought or believe in God or do good for God's sake, unless the grace of divine mercy has preceded him. We therefore believe that the glorious faith which was given to Abel the righteous, and Noah, and Abraham, and Isaac, and Jacob, and to all the saints of old, and which the Apostle Paul commends in extolling them (Heb. 11), was not given through natural goodness as it was before to Adam, but was bestowed by the grace of God. And we know and also believe that even after the coming of our Lord this grace is not to be found in the free will of all who desire to be baptized, but is bestowed by the kindness of Christ, as has already been frequently stated and as the Apostle Paul declares, "For it has been granted to you that for the sake of Christ you should not only believe in him but also suffer for his sake" (Phil. 1:29). And again, "He who began a good work in you will bring it to completion at the day of Jesus Christ" (Phil. 1:6). And again, "For by grace you have been saved through faith; and it is not your own doing, it is the gift of God" (Eph. 2:8). And as the Apostle says of himself, "I have obtained mercy to be faithful" (1 Cor. 7:25, cf. 1 Tim. 1:13). He did not say, "because I was faithful," but "to be faithful." And again, "What have you that you did not receive?" (1 Cor. 4:7). And again, "Every good endowment and every perfect gift is from above, coming down from the Father of lights" (Jas. 1:17). And again, "No one can receive anything except what is given him from heaven" (John 3:27). There are innumerable passages of holy scripture which can be quoted to prove the case for grace, but they have been omitted for the sake of brevity, because further examples will not really be of use where few are deemed sufficient.

According to the catholic faith we also believe that after grace has been received through baptism, all baptized persons have the ability and responsibility, if they desire to labor faithfully, to perform with the aid and cooperation of Christ what is of essential importance in regard to the salvation of their soul. We not only do not believe that any are foreordained to evil by the power of God, but even state with utter abhorrence that if there are those who want to believe so evil a thing, they are anathema. We also believe and confess to our benefit that in every good work it is not we who take the initiative and are then assisted through the mercy of God, but God himself first inspires in us both faith in him and love for him without any previous good works of our own that deserve reward, so that we may both faithfully seek the sacrament of baptism, and after baptism be able by his help to do what is pleasing to him. We must therefore most evidently believe that the praiseworthy faith of the thief whom the Lord called to his home in paradise, and of Cornelius the centurion, to whom the angel of the Lord was sent, and of Zacchaeus, who was worthy to receive the Lord himself, was not a natural endowment but a gift of God's kindness.

Athanasian Creed (ca. A.D. 500)

Whoever wants to be saved should above all cling to the catholic faith. Whoever does not guard it whole and inviolable will doubtless perish eternally. Now this is the catholic faith:

We worship one God in trinity and the Trinity in unity, neither confusing the persons nor dividing the divine being. For the Father is one person, the Son is another, and the Spirit is still another. But the deity of the Father, Son, and Holy Spirit is one, equal in glory, coeternal in majesty. What the Father is, the Son is, and so is the Holy Spirit. Uncreated is the Father; uncreated is the Son; uncreated is the Spirit. The Father is infinite; the Son is infinite; the Holy Spirit is infinite. Eternal is the Father; eternal is the Son; eternal is the Spirit: And yet there are not three eternal beings, but one who is eternal; as there are not three uncreated and unlimited beings, but one who is uncreated and unlimited. Almighty is the Father; almighty is the Son; almighty is the Spirit: And yet there are not three almighty beings, but one who is almighty. Thus the Father is God; the Son is God; the Holy Spirit is God: And yet there are not three gods, but one God. Thus the Father is Lord; the Son is Lord; the Holy Spirit is Lord: And yet there are not three lords, but one Lord.

As Christian truth compels us to acknowledge each distinct person as God and Lord, so catholic religion forbids us to say that there are three gods or lords. The Father was neither made nor created nor begotten; the Son was neither made nor created, but was alone begotten of the Father; the Spirit was neither made nor created, but is proceeding from the Father and the Son. Thus there is one Father, not three fathers; one Son, not three sons; one Holy Spirit, not three spirits. And in this Trinity, no one is before or after, greater or less than the other; but all three persons are in themselves, coeternal and coequal; and so we must worship the Trinity in unity and the one God in three persons. Whoever wants to be saved should think thus about the Trinity. It is necessary for eternal salvation that one also faithfully believe that our Lord Jesus Christ became flesh.

For this is the true faith that we believe and confess: That our Lord Jesus Christ, God's Son, is both God and man. He is God, begotten before all worlds from the being of the Father, and he is man, born in the world from the being of his mother—existing fully as God, and fully as man with a rational soul and a human body; equal to the Father in divinity, subordinate to the Father in humanity. Although he is God and man, he is not divided, but is one Christ. He is united because God has taken humanity into himself; he does not transform deity into humanity. He is completely one in the unity of his person, without confusing his natures. For as the rational soul and body are one person, so the one Christ is God and man.

He suffered death for our salvation. He descended into hell and rose again from the dead. He ascended into

174

heaven and is seated at the right hand of the Father. He will come again to judge the living and the dead. At his coming all people shall rise bodily to give an account of their own deeds. Those who have done good will enter eternal life, those who have done evil will enter eternal fire. This is the catholic faith. One cannot be saved without believing this firmly and faithfully.

Anathemas of the Second Council of Constantinople (A.D. 533)

I. If anyone does not confess that the Father and the Son and the Holy Spirit are one nature or essence, one power or authority, worshipped as a trinity of the same essence, one deity in three hypostases or persons, let him be anathema. For there is one God and Father, of whom are all things, and one Lord Jesus Christ, through whom are all things, and one Holy Spirit, in whom are all things.

II. If anyone does not confess that God the Word was twice begotten, the first before all time from the Father, non- temporal and bodiless, the other in the last days when he came down from the heavens and was incarnate by the holy, glorious, God-bearer, ever-virgin Mary, and born of her, let him be anathema.

III. If anyone says that God the Word who performed miracles is one and Christ who suffered is another, or says that God the Word was together with Christ who came from woman, or that the Word was in him as one person is in another, but is not one and the same, our Lord Jesus Christ, the Word of God, incarnate and become human, and that the wonders and the suffering

175

which he voluntarily endured in flesh were not of the same person, let him be anathema.

IV. If anyone says that the union of the Word of God with man was only according to grace or function or dignity or equality of honor or authority or relation or effect or power or according to his good pleasure, as though God the Word was pleased with man, or approved of him, as the raving Theodosius says; or that the union exists according to similarity of name, by which the Nestorians call God the Word Jesus and Christ, designating the man separately as Christ and as Son, speaking thus clearly of two persons, but when it comes to his honor, dignity, and worship, pretend to say that there is one person, one Son and one Christ, by a single designation; and if he does not acknowledge, as the holy Fathers have taught, that the union of God is made with the flesh animated by a reasonable and intelligent soul, and that such union is according to synthesis or hypostasis, and that therefore there is only one person, the Lord Jesus Christ one of the holy Trinity -- let him be anathema. As the word "union" has many meanings, the followers of the impiety of Apollinaris and Eutyches, assuming the disappearance of the natures, affirm a union by confusion. On the other hand the followers of Theodore and of Nestorius rejoicing in the division of the natures, introduce only a union of relation. But the holy Church of God, rejecting equally the impiety of both heresies, recognizes the union of God the Word with the flesh according to synthesis, that is according to hypostasis. For in the mystery of Christ the union according to synthesis preserves the two natures which have combined without confusion and without separation.

V. If anyone understands the expression -- one hypostasis of our Lord Jesus Christ -- so that it means the union of many hypostases, and if he attempts thus to introduce into the mystery of Christ two hypostases, or two persons, and, after having introduced two persons, speaks of one person according to dignity, honor or worship, as Theodore and Nestorius insanely have written; and if anyone slanders the holy synod of Chalcedon, as though it had used this expression in this impious sense, and does not confess that the Word of God is united with the flesh hypostatically, and that therefore there is but one hypostasis or one person, and that the holy synod of Chalcedon has professed in this sense the one hypostasis of our Lord Jesus Christ; let him be anathema. For the Holy Trinity, when God the Word was incarnate, was not increased by the addition of a person or hypostasis.

VI. If anyone says that the holy, glorious, and ever-virgin Mary is called God-bearer by misuse of language and not truly, or by analogy, believing that only a mere man was born of her and that God the Word was not incarnate of her, but that the incarnation of God the Word resulted only from the fact that he united himself to that man who was born of her; if anyone slanders the Holy Synod of Chalcedon as though it had asserted the Virgin to be God-bearer according to the impious sense of Theodore; or if anyone shall call her manbearer or Christbearer, as if Christ were not God, and shall not confess that she is truly God-bearer, because God the Word who before all time was begotten of the Father was in these last days incarnate of her, and if anyone shall not confess that in this pious sense the holy Synod of Chalcedon confessed her to be God-bearer: let him be anathema.

VII. If anyone using the expression, "in two natures," does not confess that our one Lord Jesus Christ is made known in the deity and in the manhood, in order to indicate by that expression a difference of the natures of which the ineffable union took place without confusion, a union in which neither the nature of the Word has changed into that of the flesh, nor that of the flesh into that of the Word (for each remained what it was by nature, even when the union by hypostasis had taken place); but shall take the expression with regard to the mystery of Christ in a sense so as to divide the parties, let him be anathema. Or if anyone recognizing the number of natures in the same our one Lord Jesus Christ, God the Word incarnate, does not take in contemplation only the difference of the natures which compose him, which difference is not destroyed by the union between them -- for one is composed of the two and the two are in one -- but shall make use of the number two to divide the natures or to make of them persons properly so called, let him be anathema.

VIII. If anyone confesses that the union took place out of two natures or speaks of the one incarnate nature of God the Word and does not understand those expressions as the holy Fathers have taught, that out of the divine and human natures, when union by hypostasis took place, one Christ was formed; but from these expressions tries to introduce one nature or essence of the Godhead and manhood of Christ; let him be anathema. For in saying that the only-begotten Word was united by hypostasis personally we do not mean that there was a mutual confusion of natures, but rather we understand that the Word was united to the flesh, each nature remaining what it was. Therefore there is one Christ, God and man, of the same essence with the Father as touching his Godhead, and of the same essence with us as touching his manhood. Therefore the Church of God equally rejects and anathematizes those who divide or cut apart or who introduce confusion into the mystery of the divine dispensation of Christ.

IX. If anyone says that Christ ought to be worshipped in his two natures, in the sense that he introduces two adorations, the one peculiar to God the Word and the other peculiar to the man; or if anyone by destroying the flesh, or by confusing the Godhead and the humanity, or by contriving one nature or essence of those which were united and so worships Christ, and does not with one adoration worship God the Word incarnate with his own flesh, as the Church of God has received from the beginning; let him be anathema.

X. If anyone does not confess that our Lord Jesus Christ who was crucified in the flesh is true God and the Lord of Glory and one of the Holy Trinity; let him be anathema.

XI. If anyone does not anathematize Arius, Eunomius, Macedonius, Apollinaris, Nestorius, Eutyches and Origen, together with their impious, godless writings, and all the other heretics already condemned and anathematized by the holy catholic and apostolic Church, and by the aforementioned four Holy Synods and all those who have held and hold or who in their godlessness persist in holding to the end the same opinion as those heretics just mentioned; let him be anathema.

Third Council of Constantinople (A.D. 681)

We also proclaim two natural willings or wills in him and two natural operations, without separation, without change, without partition, without confusion, according to the teaching of the holy Fathers -- and two natural wills not contrary to each other, God forbid, as the impious heretics have said they would be, but his human will following, and not resisting or opposing, but rather subject to his divine and all-powerful will. For it was proper for the will of the flesh to be moved naturally, yet to be subject to the divine will, according to the all-wise Athanasius. For as his flesh is called and is the flesh of God the Word, so also the natural will of his flesh is called and is God the Word's own will, as he himself says: "I came down from heaven, not to do my own will, but the will of the Father who sent me," calling the will of the flesh his own, as also the flesh had become his own. For in the same manner that his all-holy and spotless ensouled flesh, though divinised, was not destroyed, but remained in its own law and principle also his human will, divinised, was not destroyed, but rather preserved, as Gregory the divine says: "His will, as conceived of in his character as the Savior, is not contrary to God, being wholly divinised." We also glorify two natural operations in the same our Lord Jesus Christ, our true God, without separation, without change, without partition, without confusion, that is, a divine operation and a human operation, as the divine preacher Leo most clearly says: "For each form does what is proper to it, in communion with the other; the Word, that is, performing what belongs to the Word, and the flesh carrying out what belongs to the flesh." We will not therefore grant the existence of one natural operation of God and the creature, lest we should either raise up into the divine nature what is created, or bring down the preeminence of the divine nature into the place suitable for things that are made. For we recognize the wonders and the sufferings as of one and the same person, according to the difference of the natures of which he is and in which he has his being, as the eloquent Cyril said.

Preserving therefore in every way the unconfused and undivided, we set forth the whole confession in brief; believing our Lord Jesus Christ, our true God, to be one of the holy Trinity even after the taking of flesh, we declare that his two natures shine forth in his one hypostasis, in which he displayed both the wonders and the sufferings through the whole course of his dispensation, not in phantasm but truly, the difference of nature being recognized in the same one hypostasis by the fact that each nature wills and works what is proper to it, in communion with the other. On this principle we glorify two natural wills and operations combining with each other for the salvation of the human race.

In Darkness – Light!

Appendix 2: The Body of Christ

Since YHWH began forming a people for Himself, how man perceives and describes God has been important. In the early post-apostolic years, heresies cropped up regarding the nature of God and the person of Christ. Today, it is settled orthodoxy within the Christian faith that God is a holy trinity and Christ is fully God and fully man.

The doctrine of the trinity was the reason for the Nicaean creed of 325. The Creed of Nicaea (A.D. 325), was written mainly to refute Arianism; the teaching that Jesus was not eternal, but created. The doctrine of the Holy Trinity was at the heart of the Creed of Nicaea.

The hypostatic union was the doctrine developed by two major creeds, in response to gross errors taught by men who denied Jesus was eternally God and fully man since His incarnation. The First Council of Constantinople, (A.D. 381) and The Council of Chalcedon (A.D. 451).

There is another aspect of the nature of God that has not generated the interest that the trinity and hypostatic union have: **the body of Christ.**

Body of Christ is described in Scripture as *"heavenly Jerusalem"* (Galatians 4:26; Hebrews 12:22; and Revelations 21:9-27), *"living stones … a spiritual house for a holy priesthood"* (1 Peter 2:5); *"a chosen race, a royal priesthood, a holy nation, a people for His possession"* (1 Peter 2:9); *"saints"* and *"faithful brothers"* (Colossians 1:2). The list goes on; the point is the body of Christ consists of its varied members, all purchased by the Lord Jesus; and Christ is the head (Colossians 1:18).

We've been duped by the state-church into accepting "church" as the word describing the saints of the living God. The word "church" is not a translation of the Greek word, ekklesia; it's not even a transliteration of that word. There does not appear to be a clear record of why "church" was chosen, nor of the meaning of this word. The first known use of this word in English Bibles is found in Wycliffe's Bible, spelled "chirche." His work was translated from the Latin Vulgate and we have no clear reason for his use of this word. English Bibles after Wycliff translated "ekklesia" as "congregation" – until the Geneva Bible, which gave us "church."

The Greek word commonly presented as "church" is "*ekklesia*". Strong's Concordance defines "*ekklesia*" as "compound of <G1537> (ek) and a derivative of <G2564> (*kaleo*); a calling out, i.e. (concretely) a popular meeting, especially a religious congregation (Jewish synagogue, or Christian community of members on earth or saints in heaven or both), assembly, church."

In Smith's Bible Dictionary from 1884, page 452, we read:

> the derivation of the word 'church' is uncertain. It is found in the Teutonic and Slavonic languages and answers to the derivatives of ekklesia, which are naturally found in the romance languages and by foreign importation elsewhere. The word is generally said to be derived from the Greek *kyriakos*, meaning the lord's house. But the

derivation has been too hastily assumed. It is probably associated with the Scottish *kirk*, the Latin circus/*circulous*, the Greek *klukos*, because the congregations were gathered in circles.

Ebenezer Cobham Brewer's Dictionary of Phrase and Fable of 1898 agrees:

> The etymology of this word is generally assumed to be from the Greek, *Kuriou oikos* (house of God); but this is most improbable, as the word existed in all the Celtic dialects long before the introduction of Greek. No doubt the word means "a circle." The places of worship among the German and Celtic nations were always circular. (Welsh, *cyrch*, French, *cirque*; Scotch, *kirk*; Greek, *kirk-os*, etc.) Compare Anglo-Saxon circe, a church, with circol, a circle.

The first definition in Daniel Webster's 1828 dictionary defines "church" as "A house consecrated to the worship of God, among Christians; the Lord's house. This seems to be the original meaning of the word."

When work on the King James Bible began, the king provided 15 rules that the translators had to follow. Rule 3 is of particular interest to this topic:

> 3. The old ecclesiastical words to be kept; as the word church, not to be translated congregation, &c.

King James was separating from Rome, establishing his own state-church and translating "*ekklesia*" as "congregation" or "assembly" would have worked against the theology embraced by the state-church.

Ekklesia rendered as "congregation" or "assembly" shows we are talking about people, not places. Advocates of the state-church have a history of building geo-political empires with ostentatious buildings for their gatherings and sprinkling infants rather than baptizing disciples. Presbyterians equate Old Covenant Israel for the New Covenant saints, providing "cover" for having unconverted children as "junior" members of the local "church." Without the word "church" being properly interpreted as the called ones (or something similar), people can easily be led astray in believing a "church" is something other than the assembly of the redeemed – like a building. Missing completely the meaning intended by God.

As a bare word, *"ekklesia"* doesn't describe the purpose for which people are gathered. In Act 7:37-38 and Heb 2:11-12, *"ekklesia"* is used to describe God's covenant people in the Mosaic Covenant community.

In Acts 19:21-41, *ekklesia* is used three times to refer to townsfolk in Ephesus, showing up in English as "assembly."

In numerous passages, *"ekklesia"* refers to the saints, the redeemed in Christ, those translated from the kingdom of darkness into the kingdom of His glorious light. And we see it English as "church." Why "church" instead of "assembly" or "congregation?"

Do professing Christians grasp the meaning of "church" rightly? It's common for people to talk about "going to church," or "filling up the church," or point out "look at that beautiful church!" These and many similar phrases betray a lack of understanding of *"ekklesia."* The state-church has succeeded, we have largely lost sight of what constitutes the body of Christ.

Why does this all matter? *The ekklesia of Christ is the people of God.* Christ gave Himself for His sheep - all and each of them, whether they belong to a local congregation or are awaiting the resurrection of their bodies. He did not give Himself for any building. We who are still in our tabernacles of flesh are to love one another; in this way the world will know we are His disciples. This brotherly love within the local assembly is lost in most, as they have reduced worship to mere traditions and reduced biblical fellowship to a superficial "meet & greet" with an occasional meal. John would accuse us - how can you say you love God, Whom you cannot see, if you do not love the brother you can see? (1 John 4:20) I would add - how can you say you love your brothers and sisters in Christ if all you love are those far away, but not those with whom you rub up against and have disagreements? Jesus did not die only to provide eternal life for us; He also provided His Spirit to guide us in all truth, and in love for one another. We have been bought at a price by the One Who said:

John 15:12 (ESV) *This is my commandment, that you love one another as I have loved you.* John 15:17 (ESV) *These things I command you, so that you will love one another.*

After all, the Bible is all about the Lord Jesus and we ought to be, also. We rightly argue for and defend the Holy Trinity and the hypostatic union, even though these are difficult mysteries. We should no less careful or concerned about rightly and properly describing His Body. It's not a building, it's a redeemed people gathered into a local *ekklesia*. If we grasp this, we will more likely to stand together if persecution comes our way as it did in the Dark Ages – and continues in many places across the globe in our day.

May God grant us the grace to repent of our traditions and honor Him by talking about His body rightly, as we do in speaking of the trinity or the hypostatic union.

Bibliography

Adam, Karl; *Roots of the Reformation*, (The Coming Home Network, Zanesville, OH, USA, 2008).

Andrews, Edward D.; Christian Publishing House Blog, https://christianpublishinghouse.co/2017/03/09/the-reign-of-the-king-james-version/amp/ (accessed 7 October, 2022)

Atlas Obscura, https://www.atlasobscura.com/articles/morbid-monday-cadaver-synod (accessed 1 Sept 2022)

Bloom, Jon; "The First Tremor", https://www.desiringgod.org/articles/the-first-tremor (accessed 3 Sept 2022).

Burchett, Steve; *Wycliffe: A Bible Man in England When There Was No English Bible*, (Christian Communicators Worldwide, Parkville, MO, USA, 2022).

Busenitz, Nathan; *Long Before Luther*, (Moody Publishers, Chicago, IL, USA, 2017).

https://catholicstand.com/complete-suffering-of-christ/ (accessed 7 October, 2022)

https://www.catholic.com/encyclopedia/Kyrie-Eleison (accessed 17 March, 2023)

Christian, John T.; *A History of the Baptists, Volume I*, (Texarkana, TX, Bogard Press, 1922).

Closson, Don; "Islam & Christianity", https://probe.org/probe-powerpoint-presentations/ (accessed 27 March, 2023)

Cosmas, Sermon against Bogomilism, c. 970 AD. *Heresy and Authority in Medieval Europe*, (Peters, Edward, ed, University of Pennsylvania Press, 1980).

Cottrell, Jack; *Baptism: Zwingli or the Bible?*, (The Christian Restoration Association, Mason, OH, USA, 2022).

Cunningham, William; *Historical Theology*, (Edinburgh, Scotland, New College, 1861).

D'Aubigne, J.H. Merle; *History of the Reformation*, (Sprinkle Publications, Harrisburg, VA, USA, 2000).

Deane, David J.; *John Wicliffe, the Morning Star of the Reformation*, (S.W. Partridge & Co., London, 1884).

Duncan, Pope A.; *The Pilgrimage of Christianity*, (Nashville, TN, Broadman Press, 1965).

https://digitalcommons.liberty.edu/cgm_hist/3/ (accessed 29 March, 2023)

Hageman, Howard; *God and the Good*, (Eerdmans Publishing Company, Grand Rapids, MI, USA, 1975).

Hamlin, Talbot; *Architecture Through the Ages*, (New York, G.P. Putnam's Sons, 1953).

https://historyofchristiantheology.com/glossary/council -of-toulouse/ (accessed 7 October, 2022)

Kennedy, John W.; *The Torch of the Testimony*, (Auburn, ME, Christian Books Publishing House, 1965).

Lanier Theological Library, "Guide to the Stone Chapel," http://www.laniertheologicallibrary.net/ accessed 15 June 2013.

Meyer, Joyce; *The Most Important Decision You Will Ever Make*, (Faith Words Publishing, Murray, KY, USA, 2003).

Miller, Andrew; *Miller's Church History*, (London, UK, 1874).

Morrish, George; *Darkness of the Dark Ages*, (London, England, 1888).

https://www.merriam-webster.com/dictionary/haruspex (accessed 17 March, 2023)

Newman, John Henry; *An Essay on the Development of Christian Doctrine*, (W. Blanchard and Sons, St. Paul's, London, 1845).

http://news.bbc.co.uk/2/hi/uk_news/magazine/8375174.stm (accessed 7 October, 2022)

https://orthodoxwiki.org/Cenobitic (accessed 17 March, 2023)

Perrin, Jean Paul; *History Of The Ancient Christians*, (Brogden's Books, La Vernia, TX, USA, 2020).

https://rodiagnusdei.wordpress.com/tag/council-of-tarragona/ (Item 4, accessed 1 April, 2023)

Rone, Wendell; *The Baptist Faith and Roman Catholicism*, (Western Recorder, Middletown, KY, USA, 1952).

Schaff, David S.; *The Life of Phillip Schaff*, (Charles Scribner's Sons, New York, 1897).

Schaff, Phillip; *History of the Christian Church, Volume III: Nicene and Post-Nicene Christianity. A.D.*

311-600. (Grand Rapids, MI: Christian Classics Ethereal Library).

Schwarze, W. N.; *John Hus - The Martyr of Bohemia*, (Fleming H. Revell Company, New York, NY, USA, 1915).

Shelley, Bruce L.; *Church History in Plain Language*, (Nashville, TN, Thomas Nelson, 2008).

Smith, Matthew; Hiding Place, (Detuned Radio Music, Nashville, TN, USA, 2013), Hiding Place.

Smith, T. Roger and Slater, John; *Classic and Early Christian Architecture.*

Southern, R. W.; *Western Society and the Church in the Middle Ages* (London, UK: Pelican Books, 1970; reprint, London, UK: Penguin Books, 1990).

Sovereign Grace Music, Behold Our God, https://sovereigngracemusic.org/music/songs/behold-our-god-who-has-held-the-oceans/

https://www.thegospelcoalition.org/article/lacking-in-christs-afflictions/ (accessed 7 October, 2022)

Taylor, Isaac; *Ancient Christianity, & the doctrines of the Oxford Tracts for the times*, Dedicatory Letter (London, England, 1812).

Vedder, Henry Clay; *A Short History of the Baptists*, (Upland, PA, Crozer Theological Seminary, 1907).

Vedder, Henry Clay; *Origin and Early Teachings of the Waldenses, according to Roman Catholic Writers of the Thirteenth Century*, (The American Journal of Theology, 1900).

Verduin, Leonard; *Reformers and Their Stepchildren*, (Brogden's Books, La Vernia, TX, USA, 2020).

https://webstersdictionary1828.com/Dictionary/vicar (accessed 17 March, 2023)

Wells, Tom and Zaspell, Fred; *New Covenant Theology*, (New Covenant Media, Frederick, MD, USA, 2002).

Wellum, Stephen; *Christ Alone, the Uniqueness of Jesus as Savior*, (Zondervan Publishing, Grand Rapids, MI, 2017).

http://www.whitehorseblog.com/2020/05/13/come-hell-or-high-water-part-9/?fbclid=IwAR1lhQXrk7jG63TJ8qQSM5vj93YE6Q Z3e0WpRSkRpjSKhkl1TWDFGYzSvN8 (accessed 7 October, 2022)